Hands-On Convolutional Neural Networks with TensorFlow

Solve computer vision problems with modeling in TensorFlow and Python

Iffat Zafar
Giounona Tzanidou
Richard Burton
Nimesh Patel
Leonardo Araujo

BIRMINGHAM - MUMBAI

Hands-On Convolutional Neural Networks with TensorFlow

Copyright © 2018 Packt Publishing

Commissioning Editor: Amey Varangaonkar
Acquisition Editor: Siddharth Mandal
Content Development Editor: Aditi Gour
Technical Editor: Vaibhav Dwivedi
Copy Editor: Safis Editing
Project Coordinator: Hardik Bhinde
Proofreader: Safis Editing
Indexer: Tejal Daruwale Soni
Graphics: Jason Monteiro
Production Coordinator: Deepika Naik

First published: August 2018

Production reference: 1240818

Published by Packt Publishing Ltd.
Livery Place
35 Livery Street
Birmingham
B3 2PB, UK.

ISBN 978-1-78913-033-1

www.packtpub.com

mapt.io

Mapt is an online digital library that gives you full access to over 5,000 books and videos, as well as industry leading tools to help you plan your personal development and advance your career. For more information, please visit our website.

Why subscribe?

- Spend less time learning and more time coding with practical eBooks and Videos from over 4,000 industry professionals

- Improve your learning with Skill Plans built especially for you

- Get a free eBook or video every month

- Mapt is fully searchable

- Copy and paste, print, and bookmark content

PacktPub.com

Did you know that Packt offers eBook versions of every book published, with PDF and ePub files available? You can upgrade to the eBook version at www.PacktPub.com and as a print book customer, you are entitled to a discount on the eBook copy. Get in touch with us at service@packtpub.com for more details.

At www.PacktPub.com, you can also read a collection of free technical articles, sign up for a range of free newsletters, and receive exclusive discounts and offers on Packt books and eBooks.

Contributors

About the authors

Iffat Zafar was born in Pakistan. She received her Ph.D. from the Loughborough University in Computer Vision and Machine Learning in 2008. After her Ph.D. in 2008, she worked as research associate at the Department of Computer Science, Loughborough University, for about 4 years. She currently works in the industry as an AI engineer, researching and developing algorithms using Machine Learning and Deep Learning for object detection and general Deep Learning tasks for edge and cloud-based applications.

Giounona Tzanidou is a PhD in computer vision from Loughborough University, UK, where she developed algorithms for runtime surveillance video analytics. Then, she worked as a research fellow at Kingston University, London, on a project aiming at prediction detection and understanding of terrorist interest through intelligent video surveillance. She was also engaged in teaching computer vision and embedded systems modules at Loughborough University. Now an engineer, she investigates the application of deep learning techniques for object detection and recognition in videos.

Richard Burton graduated from the University of Leicester with a master's degree in mathematics. After graduating, he worked as a research engineer at the University of Leicester for a number of years, where he developed deep learning object detection models for their industrial partners. Now, he is working as a software engineer in the industry, where he continues to research the applications of deep learning in computer vision.

Nimesh Patel graduated from the University of Leicester with an MSc in applied computation and numerical modeling. During this time, a project collaboration with one of University of Leicester's partners was undertaken, dealing with Machine Learning for Hand Gesture recognition. Since then, he has worked in the industry, researching Machine Learning for Computer Vision related tasks, such as Depth Estimation.

Leonardo Araujo is just the regular, Brazilian, curious engineer, who has worked in the industry for the past 19 years (yes, in Brazil, people work before graduation), doing HW/SW development and research on the topics of control engineering and computer vision. For the past 6 years, he has focused more on Machine Learning methods. His passions are too many to put on the book.

Packt is searching for authors like you

If you're interested in becoming an author for Packt, please visit authors.packtpub.com and apply today. We have worked with thousands of developers and tech professionals, just like you, to help them share their insight with the global tech community. You can make a general application, apply for a specific hot topic that we are recruiting an author for, or submit your own idea.

Table of Contents

Preface

This book is all about giving a practical, hands-on introduction to machine learning with the aim of enabling anyone to start working in the field. We'll focus mainly on deep learning methods and how they can be used to solve important computer vision problems, but the knowledge acquired here can be transferred to many different domains. Along the way, the reader will also get a grip of how to use the popular deep learning library, TensorFlow.

Who this book is for

Anyone interested in a practical guide to machine learning, specifically deep learning and computer vision, will particularly benefit from reading this book. In addition, the following people will also benefit:

- Machine learning engineers
- Data scientists
- Developers interested in learning about the deep learning and computer vision fields
- Students studying machine learning

What this book covers

Chapter 1, *Setup and Introduction to Tensorflow*, covers the setting up and installation of TensorFlow along with writing a simple Tensorflow model for machine learning.

Chapter 2, *Deep Learning and Convolutional Neural Networks*, introduces you to machine learning, and artificial intelligence as well as artificial neural networks and how to train them. It also covers CNNs and how to use TensorFlow to train your own CNN.

Chapter 3, *Image Classification in Tensorflow*, talks about building CNN models and how to train them for classifying the CIFAR10 dataset. It also looks at ways to help improve the quality of our trained model by talking about different methods of initialization and regularization.

Chapter 4, *Object Detection and Segmentation*, teaches the basics of object localization, detection and segmentation and the most famous algorithms related to those topics.

Chapter 5, *VGG, Inception Modules, Residuals, and MobileNets*, introduces you to different convolutional neural network designs like VGGNet, GoggLeNet, and MobileNet.

Chapter 6, *AutoEncoders, Variational Autoencoders, and Generative Adversarial Networks*, introduces you to generative models, generative adversarial network, and different types of encoders.

Chapter 7, *Transfer Learning*, covers the usage of transfer learning and implementing it in our own tasks.

Chapter 8, *Machine Learning Best Practices and Troubleshooting*, introduces us to preparing and splitting a dataset into subsets and performing meaningful tests. The chapter also talks about underfitting and overfitting along with the best practices for addressing them.

Chapter 9, *Training at Scale*, teaches you how to train TensorFlow models across multiple GPUs and machines. It also covers best practices for storing your data and feeding it to your model.

To get the most out of this book

To get the most of the book, the reader should have some knowledge of the Python programming language and how to install some required packages. All the rest will be covered by the book with an easy language approach. Installation instructions will be given in the book and in the repository.

Download the example code files

You can download the example code files for this book from your account at www.packtpub.com. If you purchased this book elsewhere, you can visit www.packtpub.com/support and register to have the files emailed directly to you.

You can download the code files by following these steps:

1. Log in or register at www.packtpub.com.
2. Select the **SUPPORT** tab.
3. Click on **Code Downloads & Errata**.
4. Enter the name of the book in the **Search** box and follow the onscreen instructions.

Once the file is downloaded, please make sure that you unzip or extract the folder using the latest version of:

- WinRAR/7-Zip for Windows
- Zipeg/iZip/UnRarX for Mac
- 7-Zip/PeaZip for Linux

The code bundle for the book is also hosted on GitHub at `https://github.com/PacktPublishing/Hands-on-Convolutional-Neural-Networks-with-Tensorflow`. In case there's an update to the code, it will be updated on the existing GitHub repository.

We also have other code bundles from our rich catalog of books and videos available at `https://github.com/PacktPublishing/`. Check them out!

Conventions used

There are a number of text conventions used throughout this book.

`CodeInText`: Indicates code words in text, database table names, folder names, filenames, file extensions, pathnames, dummy URLs, user input, and Twitter handles. Here is an example: "Mount the downloaded `WebStorm-10*.dmg` disk image file as another disk in your system."

A block of code is set as follows:

```
import tensorflow as tf
# XOR dataset
XOR_X = [[0, 0], [0, 1], [1, 0], [1, 1]]
XOR_Y = [[0], [1], [1], [0]]
```

When we wish to draw your attention to a particular part of a code block, the relevant lines or items are set in bold:

```
import tensorflow as tf
# XOR dataset
XOR_X = [[0, 0], [0, 1], [1, 0], [1, 1]]
XOR_Y = [[0], [1], [1], [0]]
```

Any command-line input or output is written as follows:

```
$ pip install numpy
$ pip install scipy
```

Bold: Indicates a new term, an important word, or words that you see onscreen. For example, words in menus or dialog boxes appear in the text like this. Here is an example: "Select **System info** from the **Administration** panel."

Warnings or important notes appear like this.

Tips and tricks appear like this.

Get in touch

Feedback from our readers is always welcome.

General feedback: Email `feedback@packtpub.com` and mention the book title in the subject of your message. If you have questions about any aspect of this book, please email us at `questions@packtpub.com`.

Errata: Although we have taken every care to ensure the accuracy of our content, mistakes do happen. If you have found a mistake in this book, we would be grateful if you would report this to us. Please visit `www.packtpub.com/submit-errata`, selecting your book, clicking on the Errata Submission Form link, and entering the details.

Piracy: If you come across any illegal copies of our works in any form on the Internet, we would be grateful if you would provide us with the location address or website name. Please contact us at `copyright@packtpub.com` with a link to the material.

If you are interested in becoming an author: If there is a topic that you have expertise in and you are interested in either writing or contributing to a book, please visit `authors.packtpub.com`.

Reviews

Please leave a review. Once you have read and used this book, why not leave a review on the site that you purchased it from? Potential readers can then see and use your unbiased opinion to make purchase decisions, we at Packt can understand what you think about our products, and our authors can see your feedback on their book. Thank you!

For more information about Packt, please visit `packtpub.com`.

1
Setup and Introduction to TensorFlow

TensorFlow is an open source software library created by Google that allows you to build and execute data flow graphs for numerical computation. In these graphs, every node represents some computation or function to be executed, and the graph edges connecting up nodes represent the data flowing between them. In TensorFlow, the data is multi-dimensional arrays called **Tensors**. Tensors flow around the graph, hence the name TensorFlow.

Machine learning (**ML**) models, such as convolutional neural networks, can be represented with these kinds of graphs, and this is exactly what TensorFlow was originally designed for.

In this chapter, we'll cover the following topics:

- Understanding the TensorFlow way of thinking
- Setting up and installing TensorFlow
- Introduction to TensorFlow API levels
- Building and training a linear classifier in TensorFlow
- Evaluating a trained model

The TensorFlow way of thinking

Using TensorFlow requires a slightly different approach to programming than what you might be used to using, so let's explore what makes it different.

At their core, all TensorFlow programs have two main parts to them:

- Construction of a computational graph called `tf.Graph`
- Running the computational graph using `tf.Session`

In TensorFlow, a computational graph is a series of TensorFlow operations arranged into a graph structure. The TensorFlow graph contains two main types of components:

- **Operations**: More commonly called **ops**, for short, these are the nodes in your graph. Ops carry out any computation that needs to be done in your graph. Generally, they consume and produce Tensors. Some ops are special and can have certain side effects when they run.
- **Tensors**: These are the edges of your graph; they connect up the nodes and represent data that flows through it. Most TensorFlow ops will produce and consume these `tf.Tensors`.

In TensorFlow, the main object that you work with is called a Tensor. Tensors are the generalization of vectors and matrices. Even though vectors are one-dimensional and matrices are two-dimensional, a Tensor can be *n*-dimensional. TensorFlow represents Tensors as *n*-dimensional arrays of a user-specified data type, for example, `float32`.

TensorFlow programs work by first building a graph of computation. This graph will produce some `tf.Tensor` output. To evaluate this output, you must *run* it within a `tf.Session` by calling `tf.Session.run` on your output Tensor. When you do this, TensorFlow will execute all the parts of your graph that need to be executed in order to evaluate the `tf.Tensor` you asked it to run.

Setting up and installing TensorFlow

TensorFlow is supported on the latest versions of Ubuntu and Windows. TensorFlow on Windows only supports the use of Python 3, while use on Ubuntu allows the use of both Python 2 and 3. We recommend using Python 3, and that is what we will use in this book for code examples.

There are several ways you can install TensorFlow on your system, and here we will go through two of the main ways. The easiest is by simply using the pip package manager. Issuing the following command from a terminal will install the CPU-only version of TensorFlow to your system Python:

```
$ pip3 install --upgrade tensorflow
```

To install the version of Tensorflow that supports using your Nvidia GPU, simply type the following:

```
$ pip3 install --upgrade tensorflow-gpu
```

One of the advantages of TensorFlow is that it allows you to write code that can run directly on your GPU. With a few exceptions, almost all the major operations in TensorFlow can be run on a GPU to accelerate their execution speed. We will see that this is going to be essential in order to train the large convolutional neural networks described later in this book.

Conda environments

Using pip may be the quickest to get started, but I see that the most convenient method involves using conda environments.

Conda environments allow you to create isolated Python environments, which are completely separate from your system Python or any other Python programs. This way, there is no chance of your TensorFlow installation messing with anything already installed, and vice versa.

To use conda, you must download Anaconda from here: `https://www.anaconda.com/download/`. This will include conda with it. Once you've installed Anaconda, installing TensorFlow can be done by entering the certain commands in your Command Prompt. First, enter the following:

```
$ conda create -n tf_env pip python=3.5
```

This will create your conda environment with the name `tf_env`, the environment will use Python 3.5, and `pip` will also be installed for us to use.

Once this environment is created, you can start using it by entering the following on Windows:

```
$ activate tf_env
```

If you are using Ubuntu, enter the following command:

```
$ source activate tf_env
```

It should now display `(tf_env)` next to your Command Prompt. To install TensorFlow, we simply do a pip install as previously, depending on if you want CPU only or you want GPU support:

```
(tf_env)$ pip install --upgrade tensorflow
(tf_env)$ pip install --upgrade tensorflow-gpu
```

Checking whether your installation works

Now that you have installed TensorFlow, let's check whether it works correctly. In your Command Prompt, activate your environment again if it isn't already, and run Python by entering the following:

```
(tf_env)$ python
```

Now, enter the following lines into the Python interpreter to test that TensorFlow is installed correctly:

```
>>>> import tensorflow as tf
>>>> x = tf.constant('Tensorflow works!')
>>>> sess = tf.Session()
>>>> sess.run(x)
```

If everything is installed correctly, you should see the following output:

b'Tensorflow works!'

What you just typed there is the `Hello World` of TensorFlow. You created a graph containing a single `tf.constant`, which is just a constant Tensor. The Tensor was inferred to be of type string as you passed a string to it. You then created a TensorFlow Session, which is needed to run your graph and told your session to `run` on the Tensor that you created. The result of the Session running was then printed out. There is an extra `b` there because it's a byte stream that was created.

> If you don't see the aforementioned and are getting some errors, your best bet is to check the following pages for solutions to common problems experienced when installing:
> Ubuntu: https://www.tensorflow.org/install/install_linux#common_ installation_problems
> Windows: https://www.tensorflow.org/install/install_ windows#common_installation_problems

TensorFlow API levels

Before we get stuck into writing TensorFlow code, it is important to be aware of the different levels of API abstraction offered by TensorFlow in Python. This way, we can understand what is available to us when we write our code, and also we can choose the right functions or operations for the job. A lot of the time, there is little need to rewrite from scratch things that are already available for us to use in TensorFlow.

TensorFlow offers three layers of API abstraction to help write your code, and these can be visualized in the following diagram:

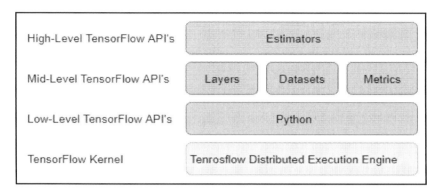

At the lowest level, you have the basic TensorFlow ops such as `tf.nn.conv2d` and `tf.nn.relu`. These low-level primitives give the user the most control when working with TensorFlow. However, using them comes at the price of having to look after a lot more things yourself when constructing a graph and writing more boilerplate code.

Don't worry about understanding any of the following code examples yet, that will come very soon I promise; it is just here now for demonstrating the different API levels in TensorFlow.

So, for example, if we want to create a convolution layer to use in our ML model, then this might look something like the following:

```
def my_conv_2d(input, weight_shape, num_filters, strides):
    my_weights = tf.get_variable(name="weights", shape=weight_shape)
    my_bias = tf.get_variable(name="bias", shape=num_filters)
    my_conv = tf.nn.conv2d(input, my_weights, strides=strides,
padding='same', name='conv_layer1')
    my_conv = tf.nn.bias_add(my_conv, my_bias)
    conv_layer_out = tf.nn.relu(my_conv)
    return conv_layer_out
```

This example is much simpler than you would actually implement, but you can already see the number of lines of code starting to build up, along with things you have to take care of such as constructing weights and adding bias terms. A model would also have many different kinds of layers, not just a convolution layer, all having to be constructed in very similar ways to this.

So, not only is it quite laborious having to write these things out for every new kind of layer you want in your model, it also introduces more areas where bugs can potentially work their way into your code which is never a good thing.

Luckily for us, TensorFlow has a second level of abstraction that helps to make your life easier when building TensorFlow graphs. One example from this level of abstraction is the layers API. The layers API allows you to work easily with many of the building blocks that are common across many machine learning tasks.

The layers API works by wrapping up everything we wrote in the previous example and abstracting it away from us, so we don't have to worry about it anymore. For example, we can condense the preceding code to construct a convolution layer into one function call. Building the same convolution layer as before would now look like this:

```
def my_conv_2d(input, kernel_size, num_filters, strides):
    conv_layer_out = tf.layers.conv2d(input, filters=num_filters,
kernel_size=kernel_size, strides=strides, padding='same',
activation=tf.nn.relu, name='conv_layer1')
    return conv_layer_out
```

There are two other APIs that work alongside layers. The first is the datasets API that provides easy loading and feeding of data to your TensorFlow graph. The second one is the metrics API that provides tools to test how well your trained machine learning models are doing. We will learn about all these later in the book.

There is one final layer to the API stack that is the highest level of abstraction that TensorFlow provides, and that is called the estimators API. In much the same way that using tf.layers took care of constructing weights and adding biases for an individual layer, the estimators API wraps up construction of many layers so that we can define a whole model, made up of multiple different layers, in one function call.

The use of the estimators API will not be covered in this book, but if the reader wishes to learn more about estimators there are some useful tutorials available on the TensorFlow website.

This book will focus on using the low-level APIs along with the layers, datasets, and metrics APIs to construct, train, and evaluate your own ML models. We believe that by getting hands-on with these lower-level APIs the reader will come out with a greater understanding of how TensorFlow works under the hood, and be better equipped to tackle a wide variety of future problems that might have to use these lower-level functions.

Eager execution

At the time of this writing, Google had just introduced the eager execution API to TensorFlow. Eager Execution is TensorFlow's answer to another deep learning library called PyTorch. It allows you to bypass the usual TensorFlow way of working where you must first define a computational graph and then execute the graph to get a result. This is known as static graph computation. Instead, with Eager Execution, you can now create the so-called dynamic graphs that are defined on the fly as you run your program. This allows for a more traditional, imperative way of programming when using TensorFlow. Unfortunately, eager execution is still under development with some features still missing, and will not be featured in this book. More information on Eager Execution can be found at the TensorFlow website.

Building your first TensorFlow model

Without further ado, let's get stuck in with building your first ML model in TensorFlow.

The problem we will tackle in this chapter is that of correctly identifying the species of Iris flower from four given feature values. This is a classic ML problem that is extremely easy to solve, but will provide us with a nice way to introduce the basics of constructing graphs, feeding data, and training an ML model in TensorFlow.

The Iris dataset is made up of 150 data points, and each data point has four corresponding features: length, petal width, sepal length, and sepal width, along with the target label. Our task is to build a model that can infer the target label of any iris given only these four features.

Let's start by loading in our data and processing it. TensorFlow has a built-in function to import this particular dataset for us, so let's go ahead and use that. As our dataset is only very small, it is practical to just load the whole dataset into memory; however, this is not recommended for larger datasets, and you will learn better ways of dealing with this issue in the coming chapters. This following code block will load our data for us, an explanation of it will follow.

```
import tensorflow as tf
import numpy as np

# Set random seed for reproducibility.
np.random.seed(0)
data, labels = tf.contrib.learn.datasets.load_dataset("iris")
num_elements = len(labels)
```

```
# Use shuffled indexing to shuffle dataset.
shuffled_indices = np.arange(len(labels))
np.random.shuffle(shuffled_indices)
shuffled_data = data[shuffled_indices]
shuffled_labels = labels[shuffled_indices]

# Transform labels into one hot vectors.
one_hot_labels = np.zeros([num_elements,3], dtype=int)
one_hot_labels[np.arange(num_elements), shuffled_labels] = 1


# Split data into training and testing sets.
train_data = shuffled_data[0:105]
train_labels = shuffled_labels[0:105]
test_data = shuffled_data[105:]
test_labels = shuffled_labels[105:]
```

Let's once again take a look at this code and see what we have done so far. After importing TensorFlow and Numpy, we load the whole dataset into memory. Our data consists of four numerical features that are represented as a vector. We have 150 total data points, so our data will be a matrix of shape 150 x 4, where each row represents a different datapoint and each column is a different feature. Each data point also has a target label associated with it, which is stored in a separate label vector.

Next, we shuffle the dataset; this is important to do, so that when we split it into training and test sets we have an even spread between both sets and don't end up with all of one type of data in one set.

One-hot vectors

After shuffling, we do some preprocessing on the data labels. The labels loaded with the dataset is just a 150-length vector of integers representing which target class each datapoint belongs to, either 1, 2, or 3 in this case. When creating machine learning models, we like to transform our labels into a new form that is easier to work with by doing something called one-hot encoding.

Rather than a single number being the label for each datapoint, we use vectors instead. Each vector will be as long as the number of different target classes you have. So for example, if you have 5 target classes then each vector will have 5 elements; if you have 1,000 target classes then each vector will have 1,000 elements. Each column in the vectors represents one of our target classes and we can use binary values to identify what class the vector is the label for. This can be done by setting all values to 0 and putting a 1 in the column for the class we want the vector label to represent.

This is easily understood with an example. For labels in this particular problem, the transformed vectors will look like this:

```
1 = [1,0,0]
2 = [0,1,0]
3 = [0,0,1]
```

Splitting into training and test sets

Finally, we take part of our dataset and put it to one side. This is known as our test set and we will not touch it until after we have trained our model. This set is used to evaluate how well our trained model performs on new data that it hasn't seen before. There are many approaches to how you should split your data up into training and test sets, and we will go into detail about them all later in the book.

For now though, we'll do a simple 70:30 split, so we only use 70% of our total data to train our model and then test on the remaining 30%.

Creating TensorFlow graphs

Now that our data is all set up, we can construct our model that will learn how to classify iris flowers. We'll construct one of the simplest machine learning models—a linear classifier, as follows:

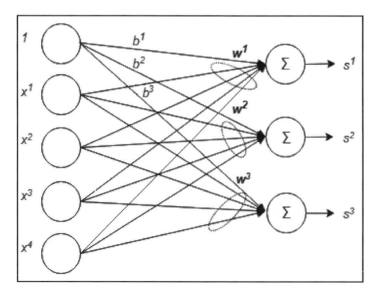

A linear classifier works by calculating the dot product between an input feature vector x and a weight vector w. After calculating the dot product, we add a value to the result called a bias term b. In our case, we have three possible classes any input feature vector could belong to, so we need to compute three different dot products with w^1, w^2, and w^3 to see which class it belongs to. But, rather than writing out three separate dot products, we can just do one matrix multiply between a matrix of weights of shape [3,4] and our input vector. In the following figure, we can see more clearly what it looks like:

$$\begin{bmatrix} w^{11} & w^{12} & w^{13} & w^{14} \\ w^{21} & w^{22} & w^{23} & w^{24} \\ w^{31} & w^{32} & w^{33} & w^{34} \end{bmatrix} \times \begin{bmatrix} x^1 \\ x^2 \\ x^3 \\ x^4 \end{bmatrix} + \begin{bmatrix} b^1 \\ b^2 \\ b^3 \end{bmatrix} = \begin{bmatrix} s^1 \\ s^2 \\ s^3 \end{bmatrix}$$

We can also just simplify this equation down to the more compact form as follows, where our weight matrix is W, bias is b, x is our input feature vector and the resulting output is s:

$$f(x; W, b) = W \cdot x + b = s$$

Variables

How do we write this all out in TensorFlow code? Let's start by creating our weights and biases. In TensorFlow, if we want to create some Tensors that can be manipulated by our code, then we need to use TensorFlow variables. TensorFlow variables are instances of the `tf.Variable` class. A `tf.Variable` class represents a `tf.Tensor` object that can have its values changed by running TensorFlow operations on it. Variables are Tensor-like objects, so they can be passed around in the same ways Tensors can and any operation that can be used with a Tensor can be used with a variable.

To create a variable, we can use `tf.get_variable()`. When you call this function, you must supply a name for your variable. This function will first check that there is no other variable with the same name already on the graph, and if there isn't, then it will create and add a new one to the TensorFlow graph.

You must also specify the shape that you want your variable to have, or alternatively, you can initialize your variable using a `tf.constant` Tensor. The variable will take the value of your constant Tensor and the shape will be automatically inferred. For example, the following will produce a 1x2 Tensor containing the values 21 and 25:

```
my_variable = tf.get_variable(name= "my_variable",
initializer=tf.constant([21, 25]))
```

Operations

It's all well and good having variables in our graph, but we also want to do something with them. We can use TensorFlow ops to manipulate our variables.

As explained, our linear classifier is just a matrix multiply so the first op you will use is funnily enough going to be the matrix multiply op. Simply call `tf.matmul()` on two Tensors you want to multiply together and the result will be the matrix multiplication of the two Tensors you passed in. Simple!

Throughout this book, you will learn about many different TensorFlow ops that you will need to use.

Now that you hopefully have a little understanding about variables and ops, let's construct our linear model. We'll define our model within a function. The function will take as input N lots of our feature vectors or to be more precise a batch of size N. As our feature vectors are of length 4, our batch will be an [N, 4] shape Tensor. The function will then return the output of our linear model. In the following code, we have written our linear model function, it should be self explanatory but keep reading if you have not completely understood it yet.

```
def linear_model(input):
# Create variables for our weights and biases
my_weights = tf.get_variable(name="weights", shape=[4,3])
my_bias = tf.get_variable(name="bias", shape=[3])

# Create a linear classifier.
linear_layer = tf.matmul(input, my_weights)
linear_layer_out = tf.nn.bias_add(value=linear_layer, bias=my_bias)
return linear_layer_out
```

In the code here, we create variables that will store our weights and biases. We give them names and supply the required shapes. Remember we are using variables as we want to manipulate their values using operations.

Next, we create a `tf.matmul` node that takes as argument our input feature matrix and our weight matrix. The result of this op can be accessed through our `linear_layer` Python variable. This result is then passed to another op, `tf.nn.bias_add`. This op comes from the **NN** (**neural network**) module and is used when we wish to add a bias vector to the result of a calculation. A bias has to be a one-dimensional Tensor.

Feeding data with placeholders

Placeholders are Tensor-like objects. They are a contract between you and TensorFlow that says when you run your computation graph in a session, you will supply or *feed* data into that placeholder so that your graph can run successfully.

They are Tensor-like objects as they behave like Tensors, meaning you can pass them around in places where you would put a Tensor.

By using placeholders, we can supply external inputs into our graph that might change each time we run our graph. The natural use for them is as a way to supply data and labels into our model as the data and labels we supply will generally be different each time we want to run our graph.

When creating a placeholder, we must supply the datatype that will be fed.

We will use two placeholders to supply data and labels into our graph. We also supply the shape that any data fed into these placeholders must take. We use None to indicate the size of that particular dimension can take any value. This way we are able to feed in batches of data that are varying sizes. Following we'll see how to define placeholders in TensorFlow for our problem.

```
x = tf.placeholder(tf.float32, shape=[None, 4], name="data_in")
y = tf.placeholder(tf.int32, shape=[None, 3], name="target_labels")
```

Now, we have created placeholders in our graph, so we can construct our linear model on the graph as well. We call our function that we defined previously, and supply as input our data placeholder, x. Remember, placeholders act like Tensors so they can be passed around like them as well. In the following code we call our linear_model function with our placeholder as the input argument.

```
model_out = linear_model(x)
```

When we call our function, everything inside it executes and all the ops and variables are added to our TensorFlow graph. We only need to do this once; if we were to try calling our function again, we would get an error saying that we have tried to add variables to the graph but they already exist.

Placeholders are the simplest and quickest way of supplying external data into our graph, so it's good to know about them. Later on, we will see better ways of supplying data using the dataset API, but for now placeholders are a good place to start.

Initializing variables

Before we are able to use our variables in our graph, we must initialize them. We need to create a graph node that will do this for us. Using `tf.global_variables_initializer` will add an initializer node to our graph. If we run this node in a session, then all the variables in our graph will become initialized so that we are able to use them. So, for now, let's create an initializer node as follows:

```
initializer = tf.global_variables_initializer()
```

As we did not explicitly say what kind of initialization to use for our variables, TensorFlow will use a default one called the Glorot Normal Initializer, which is also known as Xavier Initialization.

Training our model

We have constructed the graph of our linear model, and we can supply data into it. If we were to create a session and run the `model_out` Tensor in it while supplying some input data, then we would get a result produced. However, the output we would get would be complete rubbish. Our model has yet to be trained! The values of our weights and biases just have the default values given to them when we initialized our variables using the initializer node.

Loss functions

To train our model, we must define something called a loss function. The loss function will tell us how well or badly our model is currently doing its job.

Losses can be found in the `tf.losses` module. For this model, we will use the hinge loss. Hinge loss is the loss function used when creating a **support vector machine (SVM)**. Hinge loss heavily punishes incorrect predictions. For one given example, (x_i, y_i), where x_i is a feature vector of a datapoint and y_i is its label, the hinge loss for it will be as follows:

$$L_i = \sum_{j \neq y_i} \max(0, s_j - s_{y_j} + 1)$$

To this, the following will apply:

$$s = f(x_i; W, b) = W \cdot x_i + b$$

In simple words, this equation takes the raw output of the classifier. In our model, that's three output scores, and ensures that the score of the target class is greater, by at least 1, than the scores of the other classes. For each score (except the target class), if this restriction is satisfied, then 0 is added to the loss, otherwise, there's a penalty that is added:

$$s_j - s_{y_j} + 1$$

This concept is actually very intuitive because if our weights and biases are trained properly, then the highest of the three produced scores should confidently indicate the correct class that an input example belongs to.

Since during training we feed many training examples in at once, we'll obtain multiple losses like these that need to be averaged. Therefore, the total loss equation that needs to be minimized is as follows:

$$L = \frac{1}{N} \sum_{i=1}^{N} \sum_{j \neq y_i} \max(0, s_j - s_{y_j} + 1)$$

In our code, the loss function will take two arguments: logits and labels. In TensorFlow, logits is the name for the raw values produced by our model. In our case, this is `model_out` as this is the output of our model. For labels, we use our label placeholder, y. Remember that the placeholder will be filled for us at runtime:

```
loss = tf.reduce_mean(tf.losses.hinge_loss(logits=model_out, labels=y))
```

As we also want to average our loss across the whole batch of input data, so we use `tf.reduce_mean` to average all our losses into one loss value that we will minimize.

There are many different types of lossfunctions available for us to use that are all good for different machine learning tasks. As we go through the book, we will learn more of them and when to use different loss functions.

Optimization

Now we have defined a loss function to be used; we can use this loss function to train our model. As is shown in the previous equations, the loss function is a function of weights and biases. Therefore, all we have to do is an exhaustive search of the space of weights and biases and see which combination minimizes the loss best. When we have one- or two-dimensional weight vectors, this process might be okay, but when the weight vector space gets too big, we need a more efficient solution. To do this, we will use an optimization technique called **gradient descent**.

By using our loss function and calculus, gradient descent is able to see how to adjust the values of the weights and biases of our model in such a way that the value of the loss decreases. It is an iterative process requiring many iterations before the values of our weights and biases are well-adjusted for our training data. The idea is that the loss function L, parametrized by weights w, is minimized by updating the parameters in the opposite direction of the gradient of the objective function $\nabla_w L(w)$ with respect to the parameters. The update functions for weights and biases look like the following:

$$w_t = w_{t-1} - a\nabla_w L(w, b)$$

$$b_t = b_{t-1} - a\nabla_b L(w, b)$$

Here, t is the iteration number and α is a hyperparameter called the learning rate.

A loss function that is parameterized by two variables *w1* and *w2* will look something like in the following diagram:

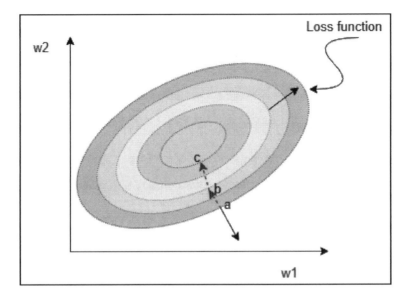

The preceding diagram shows the level curves of an elliptical paraboloid. This is a bowl-shaped surface and the bottom of the bowl lies at the center. Looking at the plot, the gradient vector at point *a* (the straight black arrow) is normal to the level curve through *a*. The gradient vector, in fact, points in the direction of the greatest rate of increase of the loss function.

So, if we start from point *a* and update the weights toward the direction *opposite* to the gradient vector, then we will descend to point *b* and in the next iteration to point *c*, and so on until we reach the minimum. The parameters that minimize the loss function are selected to represent the final trained linear model.

The nice thing about TensorFlow is it calculates all the required gradients for us using its built-in optimizers with something called **automatic differentiation**. All we have to do is choose a gradient descent optimizer and tell it to minimize our loss function. TensorFlow will automatically calculate all the gradients and then use these to update our weights for us.

We can find optimizer classes in the `tf.train` module. For now, we will use the `GradientDescentOptimizer` class, which is just the basic gradient descent optimization algorithm. When creating the optimizer, we must supply a learning rate. The value of the learning rate is a `hyperparameter` that the user must tune through trial and error and experimentation. The value of 0.5 should work well in this problem.

The optimizer node has a method called `minimize`. Calling this method on a loss function that you supply will do two things. First, gradients with respect to this loss are calculated for your whole graph. Second, these gradients are used to update all relevant variables.

Creating our optimizer node will look something like this:

```
optimizer =
tf.train.GradientDescentOptimizer(learning_rate=0.5).minimize(loss)
```

Like with loss functions, there are many different flavors of gradient descent optimizers to learn about. Presented here is the most basic kind, but again, we will learn about and use different ones in future chapters.

Evaluating a trained model

We have put together all the pieces we need in order to train our model. The last thing before we start training is that we want to create some nodes in our graph that will allow us to test how good our model has done after we have finished training it.

We will create a node that calculates the accuracy of our model.

`Tf.equal` will return a Boolean list indicating where the two supplied lists are equal. Our two lists, in this case, will be the label and the output of our model, after finding the indices of the max values:

```
correct_prediction = tf.equal(tf.argmax(model_out,1), tf.argmax(y,1))
```

We can then use `reduce_mean` again to get the average number of correct predictions. Don't forget to cast our `boolean correct_prediction` list back to `float32`:

```
accuracy = tf.reduce_mean(tf.cast(correct_prediction, tf.float32))
```

The session

Now we have constructed all the parts of our computational graph. The very final thing we need to do is create a `tf.Session` and run our graph. The TensorFlow session is a way to connect your TensorFlow program, written in Python, with the C++ runtime powering TensorFlow. The session also gives TensorFlow access to devices such as CPUs and GPUs present on your local or remote machine. In addition, the session will cache information about the constructed graph so computation can be efficiently run many times.

The standard way to create a session is to do so using a Python context manager: the `with` statement block:

```
with tf.Session() as sess:.
```

The reason for this is that when you create a session, it has control of CPU, memory, and GPU resources on your computer. When you are finished using your session, you want all these resources to be freed up again, and the easiest way to ensure this is by using a `with` statement.

The first thing we'll do after creating our session is to run our initializer op. You can evaluate nodes and Tensors in a graph using a session by calling `tf.Session.run` on the graph objects you want to evaluate. When you supply part of your graph to `session.run`, TensorFlow will work its way through the graph evaluating everything that the supplied graph part depends on in order to produce a result.

So, in our example, calling `sess.run(initializer)` will search back through the graph, find everything that is required to execute the initializer, and then execute these nodes in order. In this case, nothing is connected to the initializer node, so it will simply execute this one node that initializes all our Variables.

Now that our variables are initialized, we start the training loop. We will train for 1000 steps or iterations, so we create a for loop where our training steps will take place. The amount of steps to train for is a `hyperparameter` of sorts; it is something that we need to decide on when we train our model. There can be trade-offs with the value you choose, and this will be discussed in the future chapters. For this problem, 1000 steps will be good enough to get the desired result.

We grab a batch of training data and labels that we will feed into our graph. Next, we call `session.run` again. This time, we call it on two things, the loss and optimizer. We can supply as many things as we want to evaluate by putting them in a list that we supply to `session.run`. TensorFlow will be smart enough not to evaluate the graph multiple times if it doesn't need to, and it will reuse results that have already been calculated. This list we supply is called our fetches; it is the nodes in the graph that we want to evaluate and fetch.

After the list of fetches, we supply a `feed_dict` or feed dictionary. This is a dictionary in which each key is the Tensor in the graph that we will feed values to (in this case, our placeholders) and the corresponding value is the value that will be fed to it.

The return values of `session.run` correspond to each of the values in our fetch list. Our first fetch is the loss Tensor in our graph, so the first return argument comes from this. The second fetch is the optimizer node. We don't care about what is returned from this node as we only care about what the optimizer node calculates, so we leave its corresponding return empty:

```
with tf.Session() as sess:
    sess.run(initializer)
    for i in range(1000):
        batch_x, batch_y = train_data[:,:], train_labels[:,:]
        loss_val, _ = sess.run([loss, optimizer], feed_dict={x : batch_x,
y: batch_y})
    print("Train Accuracy:", sess.run(accuracy, feed_dict={x: train_data,
y: train_labels}))
    print("Test Accuracy:", sess.run(accuracy, feed_dict={x: test_data, y:
test_labels}))
```

After running for 1000 iterations, we use another `session.run` call to fetch the output of our accuracy node. We do this twice, once feeding in our training data to get accuracy on the training set, and once feeding in our held out test data to get the accuracy on the test set. You should get a test accuracy printed out of `0.977778`, which means our model correctly classified 44 out of 45 of our test sets, not too bad at all!

Summary

In this chapter, we have explained how programming with TensorFlow works and how to set up your work environment for working with TensorFlow. We have also looked at how to build, train, and evaluate your own linear model using TensorFlow for classifying iris flowers. In doing so, we briefly looked at loss functions and gradient descent optimizers.

In the next chapter, we will learn more about some key deep-learning concepts, including convolutional neural networks. We'll also look at how to use TensorFlow to build and train deep neural networks.

2
Deep Learning and Convolutional Neural Networks

efore we begin this chapter, we need to talk a bit about AI and **machine learning** (**ML**) and how those two components fit together. The term "artificial" refers to something that is not real or natural, whereas "intelligence" refers to something capable of understanding, learning, or able to solve problems (and, in extreme cases, being self-aware).

Officially, artificial intelligence research began at the Dartmouth Conference of 1956 where AI and its mission were defined. In the following years, everyone was optimistic as machines were able to solve algebra problems and learn English, and the first robot was constructed in 1972. However in the 1970s, due to overpromising but under delivering, there was a so-called AI winter where AI research was limited and underfunded. After this though AI was reborn through expert systems, that could display human-level analytical skills. Afterwards, a second AI winter machine learning got recognized as a separate field in the 1990s when probability theories and statistics started to be utilized.

Increases in computational power and the determination to solve specific problems led to the development of IBM's Deep Blue that beat the world chess champion in 1997 . Fast forward and nowadays the AI landscape encompasses many fields including Machine Learning, Computer Vision, Natural Language Processing, Planning Scheduling, and Optimization, Reasoning/Expert systems, and Robotics.

During the past 10 years, we have witnessed a huge transformation in what ML, and AI in general, is capable of. Thanks mainly to Deep Learning.

In this chapter, we are going to cover the following topics:

- A general explanation of the concepts of AI and ML
- Artificial neural networks and Deep Learning
- **Convolutional neural networks** (**CNN**s) and their main building blocks
- Using TensorFlow to build a CNN model to recognize images of digits
- An introduction to Tensorboard

AI and ML

For the purpose of this book, consider **artificial intelligence** (**AI**) as the field of computer science responsible for making agents (software/robots) that act to solve a specific problem. In this case, "intelligent" means that the agent is flexible and it perceives its environment through sensors and will take actions that maximize its chances to succeed at some particular goal.

We want an AI to maximize something that is named **Expected Utility** or the probability of getting some sort of satisfaction by doing an action. An easy to understand example of this is by going to school, you will maximize your expected utility of getting a job.

AI aspires to replace the error-prone human intelligence involved in completing tedious everyday tasks. Some central components of human intelligence that AI aims to mimic (and an intelligent agent should have) are:

- **Natural Language Processing** (**NLP**): Give the ability to understand spoken or written human language and give natural response to questions. Some example NLP tasks include automated narration, machine translation, or text summarization.

- **Knowledge and Reasoning**: Develop and maintain an updated knowledge of the world around the agent. Follow human reasoning and decision-making to solve specific problems and react to changes in its environment.
- **Planning and problem solving**: Making predictions about possible actions and choosing the one that maximizes some expected utility, in other words, choosing the best action for that situation.
- **Perception**: The sensors that the agent is equipped with provides it with information about the world that the agent lives in. The sensors could be something as simple as an infrared sensor or more complicated such as a microphone for speech recognition or a camera to enable machine vision.
- **Learning**: For the agent to develop knowledge of the world, it must use perception to learn through observation. Learning is a way of knowledge acquisition that will be used to reason and make decisions. The subfield of AI that deals with algorithms that learn from data without some explicit programming is named Machine Learning.

ML uses *tools* such as statistical analysis, probabilistic models, decision trees, and neural networks to process efficiently large amounts of data instead of humans.

As an example, let's consider the following problem of gesture recognition. In this example, we want our machine to identify what hand gesture is being shown. The inputs to the system are hand images, as shown in the following image, and the output is the digits that they represent. The system that would solve this problem needs to use perception in the form of vision.

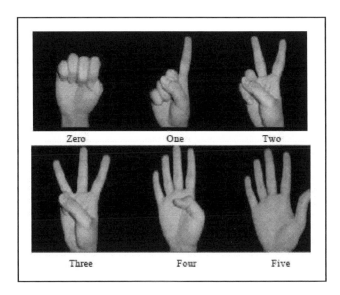

Giving just raw images as input to our machine would not produce a reasonable result. Therefore, the images should be preprocessed to extract some kind of interpretable abstraction. In our particular case, the simplest approach would be to segment the hand based on color and make a vertical projection summing the non-zero values on the x-axis. If the width of the image is 100 pixels, then the vertical projection forms a vector 100-elements long (100-dimensional), with the highest values at the location of the unfolded fingers. We can call any vector of features, that we extract, a **feature vector**.

Let's say that for our hand data, we have 1000 different images and we have now processed them to extract feature vectors for each. In the machine learning stage, all the feature vectors will be given to a machine learning system that creates a model. We hope that this model can generalize and is able to predict the digit for any future images given to the system that it wasn't trained on.

An integral part of an ML system is evaluation. When we evaluate our model, we see how well our model has done in a particular task. In our example, we would look at how accurately it can predict the digit from the image. Accuracy of 90% would mean that 90 out of 100 given images were correctly predicted. In the chapters that follow, we will discuss in more detail the machine training and evaluation process.

Types of ML

ML problems can be separated into three major groups depending on what kind of data is available to us and what we want to accomplish:

Supervised learning: Both the input and desired output or label are available to us. Hand gesture classification, where we are given images of hand gestures and corresponding labels, is an example of a supervised learning problem. We want to create a model that is able to output the correct label given an input hand image.

Supervised techniques include SVM, LDA, neural networks, CNN, K-NN, the decision tree, and so on.

Unsupervised learning: Only the inputs are available with no labels, and we don't necessarily know what we want our model to do. An example would be if we are given a large dataset containing pictures of hands, but no labels. In this case, we might know that there is some structure or relationships in the data, but we leave it up to an algorithm to try and find them within our data for us. We might want our algorithm to find clusters of similar hand gestures in our data, so we don't have to manually label them.

Another use of unsupervised learning is finding ways of reducing the dimension of the data we are using, again by finding important features in our data and discarding unimportant ones.

Unsupervised techniques include PCA, t-SNE, K-means, autoencoders, deep autoencoders, and so on.

The following image illustrates the difference between classification and clustering (when we need to find structure on unsupervised data).

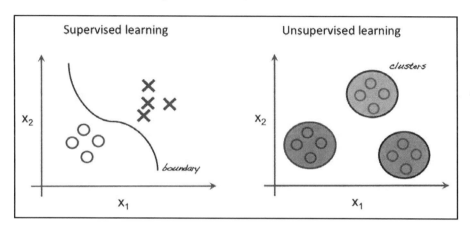

Reinforcement learning: The third kind is all about training an agent to perform some action in an environment. We know the desired outcome, but not how to get to it. Rather than having labeled data, we give the agent feedback telling it how good or bad it is at accomplishing the task. Reinforcement learning is out of the scope of this book.

Old versus new ML

The typical flow that an ML engineer might follow to develop a prediction model is as follows:

1. Gather data
2. Extract relevant features from the data
3. Choose an ML architecture (CNN, ANN, SVM, decision trees, and so on)
4. Train the model
5. Evaluate the model and repeat steps 3 to 5 until they find a satisfying solution
6. Test the model in the field

As mentioned in the previous section, the idea of ML is to have an algorithm that is flexible enough to learn the underlying process behind the data. This being said, many classic methods of ML are not strong enough to learn directly from data; they need to somehow prepare the data before using those algorithms.

We briefly mentioned it before, but this process of preparing the data is often called feature extraction, where some specialist filters out all the details of the data that we believe are relevant to its underlying process. This process makes the classification problems easier for the selected classifier as it doesn't have to work with irrelevant variables in the data that it might otherwise see as important.

The single coolest feature that new deep learning methods of ML have is they don't need (or need less of) the feature extraction phase. Instead, using large enough datasets, the model itself is capable of learning what are the best features to represent the data, directly from the data itself! The examples of these new methods are as follows:

- Deep CNNs
- Deep AutoEncoders
- **Generative Adversarial Networks** (GANs)

All these methods are a part of the deep learning process where vast amounts of data are exposed to multilayer neural networks. However, the benefits of these new methods come at a cost. All these new algorithms require much more computing resources (CPU and GPU) and could take much longer to train than traditional methods.

Artificial neural networks

Very vaguely inspired by the biological network of neurons residing in our brain, **artificial neural networks** (ANNs) are made up of a collection of units named **artificial neurons** that are organized into the following three types of layers:

- Input layer
- Hidden layer
- Output layer

The basic artificial neuron works (see the following image) by calculating a dot product between an input and its internal *weights*, and the results is then passed to a nonlinear activation function *f* (sigmoid, in this example). These artificial neurons are then connected together to form a network. During the training of this network, the aim is to find the proper set of weights that will help with whatever task we want our network to do:

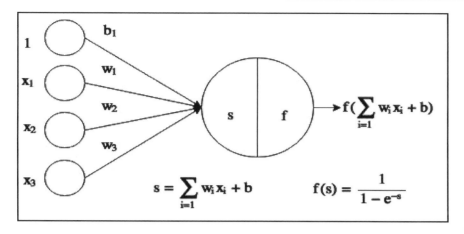

Next, we have an example of a 2-layer feed forward artificial neural network. Imagine that the connections between neurons are the weights that will be learned during training. In this example, Layer *L1* will be the input layer, *L2* the hidden layer, and *L3* the output layer. By convention, when counting the number of layers, we only include layers that have learnable weights; therefore, we do not include the input layer. This is why, it is only a 2-layer network:

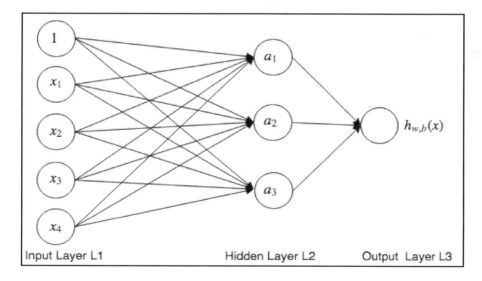

Neural networks with more than one layer are examples of nonlinear hypothesis, where the model can learn to classify much more complex relations than linear classifiers can. In fact, they are actually universal approximators capable of approximating any continuous function.

Activation functions

In order to allow the ANN models to be able to tackle more complex problems, we need to add a nonlinear block just after the neuron dot product. If we then cascade these nonlinear layers, it allows the network to compose different concepts together, making complex problems easier to solve.

The use of nonlinear activations in our neurons is very important. If we didn't use nonlinear activation functions, then no matter how many layers we cascaded we would only ever have something that behaves like a linear model. This is because any linear combination of linear functions collapses down to be a linear function.

There are a wide variety of different activation functions that can be used in our neurons, and some are shown here; the only important thing is that the functions are nonlinear. Each activation function has its own benefits and disadvantages.

Historically, it was Sigmoid and *TanH* that were the activation functions of choice for neural networks. However, these functions turned out to be bad for reliably training neural networks as they have the undesirable property that their values saturate at either end. This causes the gradients to be zero at these points, which we will find out later, and it is not a good thing when training a neural network.

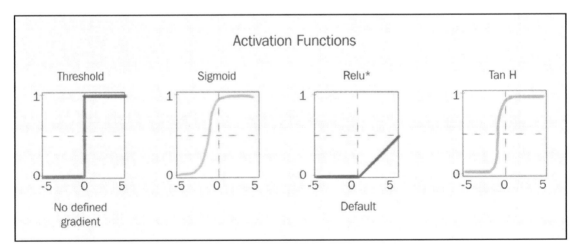

As a result, one of the more popular activation functions is the ReLU activation or **Rectified Linear Unit**. ReLU is simply a max operation between an input and 0 - max(x,0). It has the desirable property that gradients (at least at one end) will not become zero, which greatly helps the speed of convergence for neural network training.

This activation function gained popularity after it was used to help train deep CNNs. It's simplicity and effectiveness make it generally the go-to activation function to use.

The XOR problem

To explain the importance of depth in an ANN, we will look at a very simple problem that an ANN is able to solve because it has more than one layer.

In the early days of working with artificial neurons, people did not cascade layers together like we do in ANNs, so we ended up with a single layer that was named a perceptron:

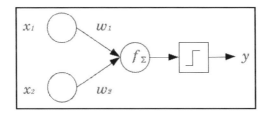

The perceptron is effectively just a dot product between an input and a set of learned weights, which means that it is actually just a linear classifier.

It was around the time of the first AI winter that people realized the weaknesses of the perceptron. As it is just a linear classifier, it is not able to solve simple nonlinear classification problems such as the Boolean exclusive-or (XOR) problem. To solve this issue, we needed to go deeper.

In this image, we see some different boolean logic problems. A linear classifier can solve the AND and OR problems but is not able to solve the XOR:

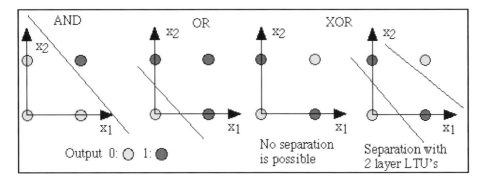

This led people to have the idea of cascading together layers of neurons that use nonlinear activations. A layer could create nonlinear concepts based on the output of the previous layer. This "composition of concepts" allows networks to be more powerful and to represent more difficult functions, and consequently, they are able to tackle nonlinear classification problems.

Training neural networks

So how do we go about setting the values of the weights and biases in our neural network that will best solve our problem? Well this is done in something called the training phase. During this phase, we want to make our neural network "learn" from a training dataset. The training dataset consists of a set of inputs (normally denoted as X) along with corresponding desired outputs or labels (normally denoted as Y).

When we say the network learns, all that is happening is the network parameters get updated in such a way that the network should be able to output the correct Y for every X in the training dataset. The expectation is that after the network is trained, it will be able to generalize and perform well for new inputs not seen during training. However, in order for this to happen, you must have a dataset that is representative enough to capture what you want to output. For example, if you want to classify cars, you need to have a dataset with different types, colors, illumination, and so on.

One common mistake when training machine learning models in general occurs when we do not have enough data or our model is not complex enough to capture the complexity of the data. These mistakes can lead to the problems of overfitting and underfitting. You will learn how to deal in practice with these problems in future chapters.

During training, the network is *executed* in two distinct modes:

- **Forward propagation**: We work forward through the network producing an output result for a current given input from the dataset. A loss function is then evaluated that tells us how well the network did at predicting the correct outputs.
- **Backward propagation**: We work backward through the network calculating the impact each weight had on producing the current loss of the network.

This image shows the two different way the network is run when training.

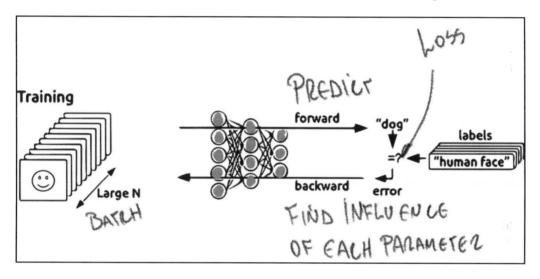

Currently, the workhorse for making neural networks "learn" is the backpropagation algorithm combined with a gradient-based optimizer like gradient descent.

Backpropagation is used to calculate gradients that tell us what effect each weight had on producing the current loss. After gradients are found an optimization technique such as gradient descent uses them to update the weights in such a way that we can minimize the value of the loss function.

 Just a closing remark: ML libraries such as TensorFlow, PyTorch, Caffe, or CNTK will provide the backpropagation, optimizers, and everything else needed to represent and train neural networks without the need to rewrite all of this code yourself.

Backpropagation and the chain rule

The backpropagation algorithm is really just an example of the trusty chain-rule from calculus. It states how to find the influence of a certain input, on systems that are composed of multiple functions. So for example in the image below, if you want to know the influence of *x* on the function *g*, we just multiply the influence of *f* on g by the influence of *x* on *f*:

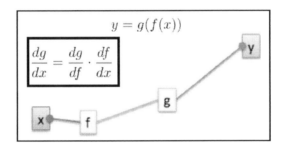

Also, this means that if we would like to implement our own deep learning library, we need to define the layers normal computation (forward propagation) and also the influence (derivative) of this computation block relative to its inputs.

Below we give some common neural network operations and what their gradients are.

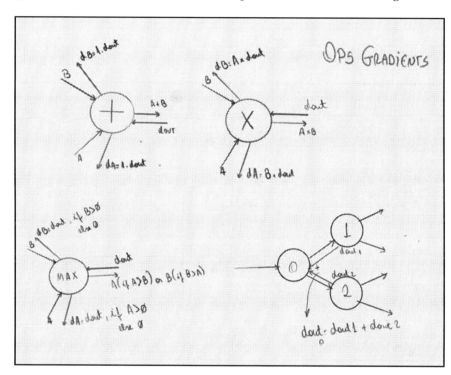

```
class MultiplyGate(object):
    # Implement Multiply gate
    def forward(self,x,y):
        z = x*y
        self.x = x;
        self.y = y;
        return z

    # Observe that we return a gradient for each input
    def backward(self,dz):
        dx = self.y * dz
        dy = self.x * dz
        return [dx,dy]

class AddGate(object):
    # Implement Add gate
    def forward(self,x,y):
        z = x+y
        self.x = x;
        self.y = y;
        return z

    # Observe that we return a gradient for each input
    def backward(self,dz):
        dx = 1*dz
        dy = 1*dz
        return [dx,dy]
```

```
In [2]: import gatesUtils as gates

In [3]: gateMul = gates.MultiplyGate(); gateAdd = gates.AddGate();

In [4]: gateAdd.forward(5,6)
Out[4]: 11

In [5]: gateMul.forward(2,3)
Out[5]: 6

In [6]: gateMul.backward(2)
Out[6]: [6, 4]

In [7]: gateAdd.backward(3)
Out[7]: [3, 3]
```

Batches

The idea of having the whole dataset in memory to train networks, as the example in Chapter 1, *Setup and Introduction to TensorFlow*, is intractable for large datasets. What people do in practice is, during training, they divide the dataset into small pieces, named mini batches (or commonly just batches). Then, in turn, each mini batch is loaded and fed to the network where the backpropagation and gradient descent algorithms will be calculated and weights then updated. This is then repeated for each mini batch until you have gone through the dataset completely.

The gradient calculated for a mini-batch is a noisy estimate of the true gradient of the whole training set, but by repeatedly getting these small noisy updates, we will still eventually converge close enough to a good minimum of the loss function.

Bigger batch sizes give a better estimate of the true gradient. Using a larger batch size will allow for a larger learning rate. The trade-off is that more memory is required to hold this batch while training.

When the model has seen your entire dataset then we say that an epoch has been completed. Due to the stochastic nature of training you will want to train your models for multiple epochs as it is unlikely for your model to have converged in only one epoch.

Loss functions

During the training phase, we need to correctly predict our training set with our current set of weights; this process consists of evaluating our training set inputs X and comparing with the desired output Y. Some sort of mechanism is needed to quantify (return a scalar number) on how good our current set of weights are in terms of correctly predicting our desired outputs. This mechanism is named the **loss function.**

The backpropagation algorithm should return the derivative of each parameter with respect to the loss function. This means we find out how changing each parameter will affect the value of the loss function. It is then the job of the optimization algorithm to minimize the loss function, in other words, make the training error smaller as we train.

One important aspect is to choose the right loss function for the job. Some of the most common loss functions and what tasks they are used for are given here:

- **Log Loss** - Classification tasks (returning a label from a finite set) with only two possible outcomes
- **Cross-Entropy Loss** - Classification tasks (returning a label from a finite set) with more than two outcomes
- **L1 Loss** - Regression tasks (returning a real valued number)
- **L2 Loss** - Regression tasks (returning a real valued number)
- **Huber Loss** - Regression tasks (returning a real valued number)

We will see different examples of loss functions in action throughout this book.

Another important aspect of loss functions is that they need to be differentiable; otherwise, we cannot use them with backpropagation. This is because backpropagation requires us to be able to take the derivative of our loss function.

In the following diagram, you can observe that the loss function is connected at the end of the neural network (model output) and basically depends on the output of the model and the dataset desired targets.

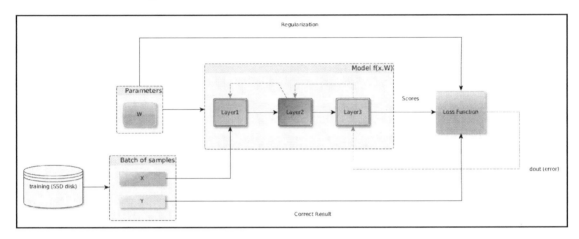

This is also shown in the following line of code in TensorFlow as the loss only needs labels and outputs (called logits here).

```
loss = tf.losses.sparse_softmax_cross_entropy(labels=labels, logits=logits)
```

You probably noticed a third arrow also connected to the loss function. This is related to something named regularization, which will be explored in Chapter 3, *Image Classification in TensorFlow*; so for now, you can safely ignore it.

The optimizer and its hyperparameters

As mentioned before, the job of the optimizer is to update the network weights in a way that is going to minimize the training loss error. In all deep learning libraries such as TensorFlow, there is only really one family of optimizer used and that is the gradient descent family of optimizers.

The most basic of these is simply called gradient descent (sometimes called vanilla gradient descent), but more complex ones that try to improve on it have been developed. Some popular ones are:

- Gradient descent with momentum
- RMSProp
- Adam

All of TensorFlow's different optimizers can be found in the `tf.train` class. For example the Adam optimizer can be used by calling `tf.train.AdamOptimizer()`.

As you may suspect, they all have configurable parameters that control how they work, but usually the most important one to pay attention to and change is as follows:

- Learning rate: Control how quickly your optimizer tries to minimize the loss function. Set it too high and you will have problems converging to a minimum. Set it too small and it will take forever to converge or get trapped in a bad local minimum.

The following image shows the problems of having a badly chosen learning rate can have:

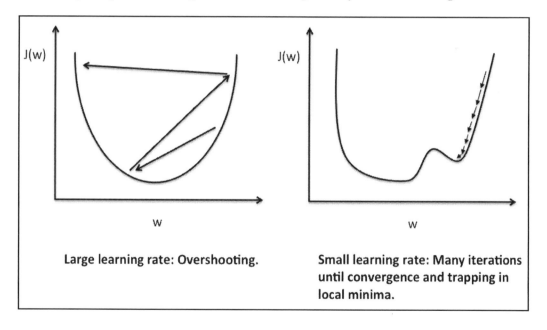

Large learning rate: Overshooting.

Small learning rate: Many iterations until convergence and trapping in local minima.

Another important aspect of the learning rate is that as your training progresses and the error drops, the learning rate value that you chose at the beginning of the training might become too big, and so you may start to overshoot the minimum.

To solve this issue, you may schedule a learning rate decay that from time to time decrease the learning rate as you train. This process is called **learning rate scheduling**, and there are several popular approaches that we will discuss in detail in the next chapter.

An alternative solution is to use one of the adaptive optimizers such as Adam or RMSProp. These optimizers have been designed so that they automatically adjust and decay the learning rates for all your model parameters as you train. This means that in theory you shouldn't have to worry about scheduling your own learning rate decay.

Ultimately you want to choose the optimizer that will train your network fastest and to the best accuracy. The following image shows how the choice of optimizer can affect the speed at which your network converges. There can be quite a gap between different optimizers, and this might change for different problems, so ideally if you can you should try out all of them and find what works best for your problem.

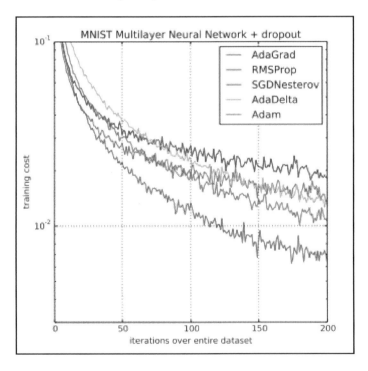

However, if you don't have time to do this, then the next best approach is to first try Adam as an optimizer as it generally works very well with little tuning. Then, if you have time, try SGD with Momentum; this one will take a bit more tuning of parameters such as learning rate, but it will generally produce very good results when well tuned.

Underfitting versus overfitting

When designing a neural network to solve a specific problem, we may have lots of moving parts, and have to take care of many things at the same time such as:

- Preparing your dataset
- Choosing the number of layers/number of neurons
- Choosing optimizer hyper-parameters

If we focus on the second point, it leads us to learn about two problems that might occur when choosing or designing a neural network architecture/structure.

The first of these problems is if your model is too big for the amount, or complexity, of your training data. As the model has so many parameters, it can easily just learn exactly what it sees in your training set even down to the noise that is present in the data. This is a problem because when the network is presented with data that is not exactly like the training set, it will not perform well because it has learned too precisely what the data looks like and has missed the bigger picture behind it. This issue is called **overfitting** or having **high-variance**.

On the other hand, you might choose a network that is not big enough to capture the data complexity. We now have the opposite problem, and your model is unable to capture the underlying structure behind your dataset well enough as it doesn't have the capacity (parameters) to fully learn. The network will again not be able to perform well on new data. This issue is called **underfitting** or having **high-bias**.

As you may suspect, you will always be looking for the right balance when it comes to your model complexity to avoid these issues.

In later chapters, we will see how to detect, avoid, and remedy those problems, but just for the sake of introduction, these are some of the classic ways to solve these issues:

- Getting more data
- Stopping when you detect that the error on the test data starts to grow (early-stopping)
- Starting the model design as simple as possible and only adding complexity when you detect underfitting

Feature scaling

In order to make the life of the optimizer algorithms easier, there are some techniques that can and should be applied to your data as an initial step before training and testing.

If the values on different dimensions of your input vector are out of scale with each other, your loss space will be somehow stretched. This will make it harder for the gradient descent algorithm to converge or at least make it slower to converge.

This normally happens when the features of your dataset are out of scale. For example, a dataset about houses might have "number of rooms" as one feature in your input vector that could have values between 1 and 4, whereas another feature might be "house area", and this could be between 1000 and 10000. Obviously, these are hugely out of scale of each other and this can make learning difficult.

In the following picture, we see a simple example of what our loss function might look like if our input features are not all in scale with each other and what it might look like when they are properly scaled. Gradient descent has a harder time reaching the minimum of the loss function when data is badly scaled.

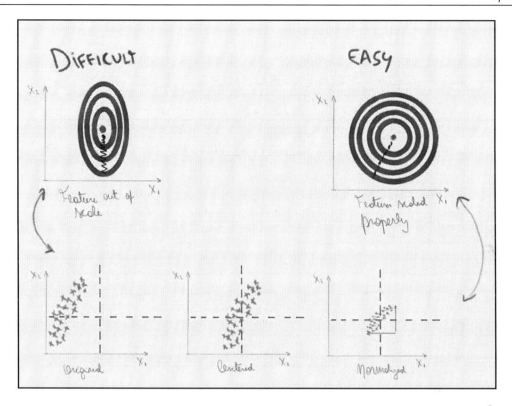

Normally, you would do some standardization of the data, such as subtract the mean and divide by the standard deviation of your dataset before using it. In the case of RGB images, it's usually enough to just subtract 128 from each pixel value to center the data around zero. However, a better approach would be to calculate the mean pixel value for each image channel in your dataset. You now have three values, one for each image channel, which you now take away from your input images. We don't really need to worry about scaling when dealing with images as all features have the same scale (0-255) to start with.

Very very important to remember - if you do some preprocessing of your data at train time, you must do this exact same preprocessing at test time otherwise expect to get some bad results!

Fully connected layers

The layers of neurons that make up the ANNs that we saw earlier are commonly called densely connected layers, or **fully connected** (**FC**) layers or simply just linear layers. Some deep learning libraries such as Caffe would actually consider them just as the dot product operation that might or might not be followed by a nonlinearity layer. Its main parameter will be the output size, which will be basically the number of neurons in its output.

In `Chapter 1`, *Setup and Introduction to TensorFlow*, we created our own dense layer, but you can create it in an easier way using `tf.layers`, as follows:

```
dense_layer = tf.layers.dense(inputs=some_input_layer, units=1024,
activation=tf.nn.relu)
```

Here, we defined a fully connected layer with 1,024 outputs, and it will be followed by a ReLU activation.

It is important to note that the input of this layer has to have just two dimensions, so if your input is a spatial tensor for example an image of shape [28*28*3] you will have to reshape it into a vector before inputting it :

```
reshaped_input_to_dense_layer = tf.reshape(spatial_tensor_in, [-1, 28 * 28
* 3])
```

A TensorFlow example for the XOR problem

Here, we put together some of the things we have learned about so far and will solve the Boolean XOR problem with TensorFlow. In this example, we are going to create a three-layer neural network with sigmoid activation functions. We use log loss as there is only two possible outcomes for out network 0 or 1:

```
import tensorflow as tf
# XOR dataset
XOR_X = [[0, 0], [0, 1], [1, 0], [1, 1]]
XOR_Y = [[0], [1], [1], [0]]

num_input = 2
num_classes = 1

# Define model I/O (Placeholders are used to send/get information from
graph)
x_ = tf.placeholder("float", shape=[None, num_input], name='X')
y_ = tf.placeholder("float", shape=[None, num_classes], name='Y')
```

```
# Model structure
H1 = tf.layers.dense(inputs=x_, units=4, activation=tf.nn.sigmoid)
H2 = tf.layers.dense(inputs=H1, units=8, activation=tf.nn.sigmoid)
H_OUT = tf.layers.dense(inputs=H2, units=num_classes,
activation=tf.nn.sigmoid)

# Define cost function
with tf.name_scope("cost") as scope:
   cost = tf.losses.log_loss( labels=y_, predictions=H_OUT)
   # Add loss to tensorboard
   tf.summary.scalar("log_loss", cost)

# Define training ops
with tf.name_scope("train") as scope:
   train_step = tf.train.GradientDescentOptimizer(0.1).minimize(cost)

merged_summary_op = tf.summary.merge_all()

# Initialize variables(weights) and session
init = tf.global_variables_initializer()
sess = tf.Session()
# Configure summary to output at given directory
writer = tf.summary.FileWriter("./logs/xor_logs", sess.graph)
sess.run(init)

# Train loop
for step in range(10000):
   # Run train_step and merge_summary_op
   _, summary = sess.run([train_step, merged_summary_op], feed_dict={x_:
XOR_X, y_: XOR_Y})
   if step % 1000 == 0:
       print("Step/Epoch: {}, Loss: {}".format(step, sess.run(cost,
feed_dict={x_: XOR_X, y_: XOR_Y})))
       # Write to tensorboard summary
       writer.add_summary(summary, step)
```

If you run this script, you should expect to get the following loss graph. We can see the loss has gone to zero that shows the model is trained and has solved the problem. You can repeat this experiment, but now only have one dense layer; you should notice, as we said, that the model is not able to solve the problem

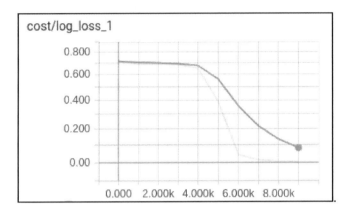

To be able to view the graph, you can run the following command in your Command Prompt from the directory where your script is located. This will launch tensorboard for us. We will find out more about tensorboard later in this chapter.

```
$ tensorboard --logdir=./logs/xor_logs
```

Convolutional neural networks

We will now look at another type of neural network that is especially designed to work with data that has some spatial properties, such as images. This type of neural network is called a **Convolutional Neural Network (CNN)**.

A CNN is mainly composed of layers called **convolution layers** that filter their layer inputs to find useful features within those inputs. This filtering operation is called convolution, which gives rise to the name of this kind of neural network.

The following diagram shows the 2-D convolution operation on an image and its result. It is important to remember that the filter kernel has a depth that matches the depth of the input (3 in this case):

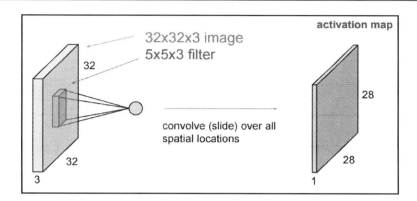

It is also important to be clear that an input to a convolution layer doesn't have to be a 1 or 3 channel image. Input tensors to a convolution layer can have any amount of channels.

 A lot of the time when talking about convolution layers in a CNN people like to shorten the word convolution down to conv. This is extremely common practice and we will also do the same in this book.

Convolution

The convolution operation is a linear operation, represented by an asterisk, that merges two signals:

$$f[x,y] * g[x,y] \;=\; \sum_{n_1=-\infty}^{\infty} \sum_{n_2=-\infty}^{\infty} f[n_1,n_2] \cdot g[x-n_1,y-n_2]$$

Two-dimensional convolutions are used in image processing to implement image filters, for example, to find a specific patch on an image or to find some feature in an image.

In CNNs, the convolutional layers filter an input tensor in a tile like fashion with a small window called a **kernel**. The kernel is what defines exactly the things a convolution operation is going to filter for and will produce a strong response when it finds what it's looking for.

The following figure shows the result of convolving an image with a particular kernel called a Sobel Filter that is good for finding edges in an image:

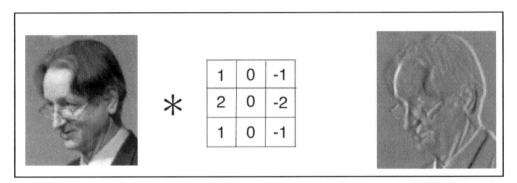

As you might have guessed, the parameters to be learned in a convolution layer are the weights of a layer's kernel. During the training of CNN, the values of these filters are adjusted automatically in order to extract the most useful information for the task at hand.

In traditional neural networks, we would have to convert any input data to a single one-dimensional vector, thus losing all the important spatial information after this vector is sent to a fully connected layer. Moreover, each pixel would have a parameter per neuron leading to an explosion in the number of parameters in a model with any large input size or depth.

However, in the case of a convolution layer, each kernel will slide across the entire input "searching" for specific patches. Kernels in CNNs are small in size and independent of the size of what they convolving. As a result, the expense of using conv layers, in terms of parameters, is generally much less than compared to the traditional dense layers we learnt about earlier.

The following figure shows the difference between a traditional fully connected layer and a convolutional (locally connected) layer. Note the huge difference in parameters:

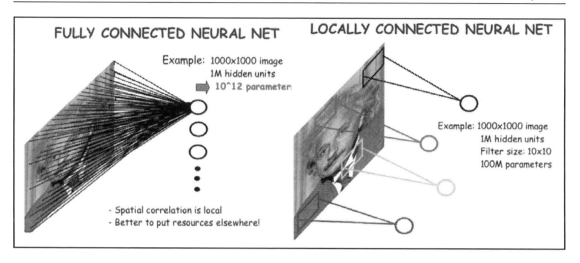

Now, perhaps we want our convolution layer to look for six different things in its input instead of just one. In this case, we will just give the convolution layer six filters of the same size (5x5x3 in this case) instead of just one. Each conv filter will then look for a particular pattern in the input.

The input and output for this particular six filter convolution layers is shown in the following diagram:

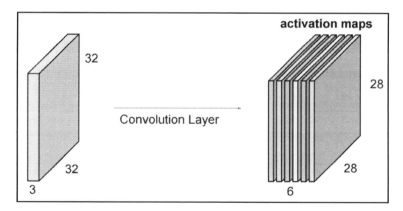

The main hyperparameters that control the behavior of the convolution layer are as follows:

- **Kernel size (K)**: How big your sliding windows are in pixels. Small is generally better and usually odd value such as 1,3,5 or sometimes rarely 7 are used.
- **Stride (S)**: How many pixels the kernel window will slide at each step of convolution. This is usually set to 1, so no locations are missed in an image but can be higher if we want to reduce the input size down at the same time.
- **Zero padding (pad)**: The amount of zeros to put on the image border. Using padding allows the kernel to completely filter every location of an input image, including the edges.
- **Number of filters (F)**: How many filters our convolution layer will have. It controls the number of patterns or features that a convolution layer will look for.

In TensorFlow, we would find the the 2-D convolution layer in the `tf.layers` module, and it can be added to your model as follows:

```
conv1 = tf.layers.conv2d(
    inputs=input_layer,
    filters=32,
    kernel_size=[5, 5],
    padding="same",
    activation=tf.nn.relu)
```

Input padding

If we did nothing, then the convolution operation will output a result that is spatially smaller than the input to it. To avoid this effect and to ensure that our convolution kernel looks at every image location, we can place zeros on the border of our input image. When we do this, we are said to be padding the image:

Zero Padding the border

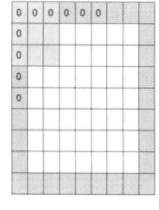

e.g. input 7x7
3x3 filter, applied with **stride 1**
pad with 1 pixel border => what is the output?

7x7 output!
in general, common to see CONV layers with
stride 1, filters of size FxF, and zero-padding with
(F-1)/2. (will **preserve size spatially**)
e.g. F = 3 => zero pad with 1
F = 5 => zero pad with 2
F = 7 => zero pad with 3

Fig Credit: A Karpathy, CS231n

The TensorFlow convolution operations provide you with two options for your padding needs: same and valid.

- Valid - TensorFlow does not pad the image. Your convolution kernels will only go to "valid" places in the input.
- Same - If we assume stride is one, then in this case, TensorFlow will pad the input enough so that the output spatial size is the same as the input spatial size.

If you really wish to have more control of your padding, you can use `tf.pad()` on the input to a layer to pad your input with exactly how many zeros you want.

In general, we can calculate the output size of a convolution operation using the following formulas:

$$H_{out} = 1 + \frac{H_{in} + (2.pad) - K_{height}}{S}, \quad W_{out} = 1 + \frac{W_{in} + (2.pad) - K_{width}}{S}$$

(Here, pad is the number of zeros added to each border.)

However in TensorFlow, because of the nature of the valid and same padding options, the formulas become as follows:

```
# Same padding
out_height = ceil(float(in_height) / float(strides[1]))
 out_width  = ceil(float(in_width) / float(strides[2]))
 # Valid padding
 out_height = ceil(float(in_height - filter_height + 1) /
float(strides[1]))
 out_width  = ceil(float(in_width - filter_width + 1) / float(strides[2]))
```

Calculating the number of parameters (weights)

Here, we will show how to calculate the number of parameters used by a convolution layer. The formula to calculate the number of parameters in a convolution layer (including biases) is as follows:

$$n_{params} = ((F.F.depth_{input}) + 1).num_{filters}$$

We will illustrate with a simple example:

```
Input: [32x32x3] input tensor
Conv layer: Kernel:5x5
            numFilters:10
```

$$n_{params} = ((5 * 5 * 3) + 1) * 10 = 760$$

On the other hand, the number of parameters in a fully connected layer (including biases) will be as follows:

$$n_{params} = (input_{tensor_{shape}} * num_{outputs})$$

As mentioned before, if you use a traditional artificial neural network directly on the image, all the spatial information will be lost and you will have an explosion of parameters as you will have one parameter per pixel per neuron. Using the same example mentioned previously and with a dense layer of 10 output neurons, we get the following numbers:

$$n_{params} = ([32 * 32 * 3] + 1) * 10 = 30730$$

This demonstrates the order of magnitude difference in parameters between these two layer types.

Calculating the number of operations

Now we're interested in calculating the computational cost of a particular convolution layer. This step is important if you would like to understand how to implement efficient network structures, perhaps when speed is key like in mobile devices. Another reasons is to see how many multipliers are needed to implement a particular layer in hardware. The convolutional layers in modern CNN architectures can be responsible for up to 90% of all computation in the model!

These are the factors that impact the number of MACs (Multiply add accumulators)/operations:

- Convolution kernel size (F)
- Number of filters (M)
- Height and Width of the input feature map (H,W)
- Input batch size (B)
- Input depth size (channels) (C)
- Convolution layer stride (S)

The number of MACs can then be calculated as:

$$\#MAC=[F*F*C*(H+2*P-FS+1)*(W+2*P-FS+1) * M]* B$$

For example, let's consider a conv layer with input 224 x 224 x 3, batch size 1, kernel 3x3, 64 filters, stride 1, and pad 1:

$$\#MAC=3*3*(224+2-31+1)*(224+2-31+1) * 3 * 64 * 1=9,462,528$$

In contrast, the fully connected layer has the following number of operations:

#MAC=[H*W*C*Outputneurons]*B

Let's reuse the same example but now with a dense layer of 64 neurons:

#MAC=[224*224*3*64]*1=9,633,792

(We have excluded biases for all op calculations, but they shouldn't add too much cost.)

 Generally in a CNN the early conv layers contribute most of the computation cost but have the least parameters. Towards the end of the network it is reversed with later layers having more parameters but costing less computationally.

Converting convolution layers into fully connected layers

Actually, we can consider fully connected layers as a subset of convolution layers. It's possible to convert a CNN layer into a fully connected layer if we set the kernel size to match the input size. Setting the number of filters is then the same as setting the number of output neurons in a fully connected layer. Check for yourself that in this case, the operations will be the same.

Example:

Consider an FC layer with 4,096 output neurons and input of size 7x7x512, the conversion would be:

Conv layer: Kernel:7x7, Pad:0, Stride:1, Filters:4,096.

Using the formula to calculate output size, we get an output of size 1 x 1 x 4096.

One of the main reason for doing this is so that your network becomes fully convolutional. When your network is fully convolutional, it doesn't matter if you decide to use a bigger input size image than what you trained on as you don't have any fully connected layers that require a fixed input size.

The pooling layer

The **pooling layer** is used to reduce the spatial dimensions of our activation tensors, but not volume depth, in a CNN. They are non parametric way of doing this, meaning that the pooling layer has no weights in it. Basically, the following is what you gain from using pooling:

- Cheap way of summarizing spatially related information in an input tensor
- By having less spatial information, you gain computation performance
- You get some translation invariance in your network

However one of the big advantage of pooling, that it has no parameters to learn, is also its biggest disadvantage because pooling can end up just throwing important information away. As a result, pooling is starting to be used less frequently in CNNs now.

In the diagram here, we show the most common type of pooling the max-pooling layer. It slides a window, like a normal convolution, and then at each location, sets the biggest value in the window as the output:

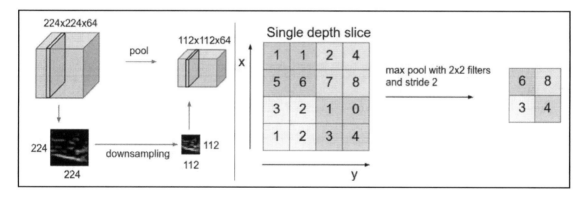

In TensorFlow, we can define pooling layers like this:

```
tf.layers.max_pooling2d(inputs=some_input_layer, pool_size=[2, 2],
strides=2)
```

1x1 Convolution

This type of convolution initially might seem a bit odd, but the 1x1 convolutions are actually used to adapt depths, by merging them, without changing the spatial information. We use this type of convolution when we need to transform a volume depth into another (called squeezing or expanding) without losing spatial information:

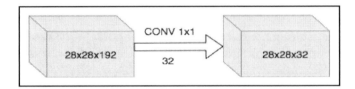

Calculating the receptive field

The receptive field is how much a particular convolution window "sees" of its input tensor.

Sometimes, it might be useful to know exactly how much each pixel in the activation from a particular layer "sees" in the input image; this is particularly important in object detection systems because we need to somehow see how some layers activations map back to the original image size.

In the following image we can see that the receptive field of a three sequential 3x3 convolution layers is the same as one 7x7 convolution layer. This property was important when designing new and better CNN models as we will see in later chapters.

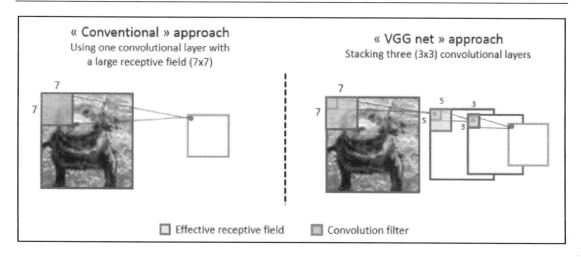

The receptive field can be calculated as:

$$R_k = R_{k-1} + ((Kernel_k - 1).\prod_{i=1}^{k-1} s_i)$$

Here, the components are as follows:

- R_k: Receptive field of layer k
- $Kernel_k$: Kernel size at layer k
- s_i: Strides from layer i (1..k-1)
- $\prod_{i=1}^{k-1} s_i$: Product of all strides up to the layer k-1 (all previous layers and not the current one)

For the first layer only, the receptive field is just the kernel size.

Those calculations are independent on if we are using convolution or pooling layer, for example, a conv layer with stride 2 will have the same receptive field as a pooling layer with stride 2.

For instance, given a 14x14x3 image after the following layers, this will apply:

- CONV: S:1, P:0, K:3
- CONV: S:1, P:0, K:3
- Max pool: S:2, P:0, K2
- CONV: S:1, P:0, K:3

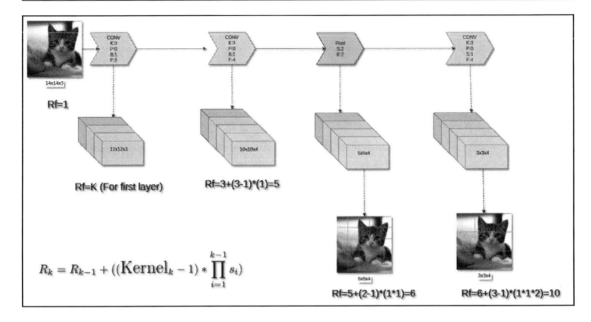

$$R_k = R_{k-1} + ((\text{Kernel}_k - 1) * \prod_{i=1}^{k-1} s_i)$$

Building a CNN model in TensorFlow

Before we start, there is a bit of good news: using TensorFlow, you don't need to take care about writing backpropagation or gradient descent code and also all common types of layers are already implemented, so things should be easier.

In the TensorFlow example here, we will change things a bit from what you learned in Chapter 1, *Setup and Introduction to TensorFlow*, and use the tf.layers API to create whole layers of our network with ease:

```
import tensorflow as tf
from tensorflow.examples.tutorials.mnist import input_data
mnist = input_data.read_data_sets("MNIST_data/", one_hot=True)
# MNIST data input (img shape: 28*28)
num_input = 28*28*1
# MNIST total classes (0-9 digits)
num_classes = 10


# Define model I/O (Placeholders are used to send/get information from
graph)
x_ = tf.placeholder("float", shape=[None, num_input], name='X')
y_ = tf.placeholder("float", shape=[None, num_classes], name='Y')
# Add dropout to the fully connected layer
is_training = tf.placeholder(tf.bool)
```

```
# Convert the feature vector to a (-1)x28x28x1 image
# The -1 has the same effect as the "None" value, and will
# be used to inform a variable batch size
x_image = tf.reshape(x_, [-1, 28, 28, 1])


# Convolutional Layer #1
# Computes 32 features using a 5x5 filter with ReLU activation.
# Padding is added to preserve width and height.
# Input Tensor Shape: [batch_size, 28, 28, 1]
# Output Tensor Shape: [batch_size, 28, 28, 32]
conv1 = tf.layers.conv2d(inputs=x_image, filters=32, kernel_size=[5, 5],
padding="same", activation=tf.nn.relu)


# Pooling Layer #1
# First max pooling layer with a 2x2 filter and stride of 2
# Input Tensor Shape: [batch_size, 28, 28, 32]
# Output Tensor Shape: [batch_size, 14, 14, 32]
pool1 = tf.layers.max_pooling2d(inputs=conv1, pool_size=[2, 2], strides=2)


# Convolutional Layer #2
# Computes 64 features using a 5x5 filter.
# Input Tensor Shape: [batch_size, 14, 14, 32]
# Output Tensor Shape: [batch_size, 14, 14, 64]
conv2 = tf.layers.conv2d( inputs=pool1, filters=64, kernel_size=[5, 5],
padding="same", activation=tf.nn.relu)


# Pooling Layer #2
# Second max pooling layer with a 2x2 filter and stride of 2
# Input Tensor Shape: [batch_size, 14, 14, 64]
# Output Tensor Shape: [batch_size, 7, 7, 64]
pool2 = tf.layers.max_pooling2d(inputs=conv2, pool_size=[2, 2], strides=2)


# Flatten tensor into a batch of vectors
# Input Tensor Shape: [batch_size, 7, 7, 64]
# Output Tensor Shape: [batch_size, 7 * 7 * 64]
pool2_flat = tf.reshape(pool2, [-1, 7 * 7 * 64])


# Dense Layer
# Densely connected layer with 1024 neurons
# Input Tensor Shape: [batch_size, 7 * 7 * 64]
# Output Tensor Shape: [batch_size, 1024]
dense = tf.layers.dense(inputs=pool2_flat, units=1024,
activation=tf.nn.relu)


# Add dropout operation; 0.6 probability that element will be kept
dropout = tf.layers.dropout( inputs=dense, rate=0.4, training=is_training)


# Logits layer
```

```
# Input Tensor Shape: [batch_size, 1024]
# Output Tensor Shape: [batch_size, 10]
logits = tf.layers.dense(inputs=dropout, units=10)

# Define a loss function (Multinomial cross-entropy) and how to optimize it
cross_entropy =
tf.reduce_mean(tf.nn.softmax_cross_entropy_with_logits(logits=logits,
labels=y_))
train_step = tf.train.AdamOptimizer(1e-4).minimize(cross_entropy)

correct_prediction = tf.equal(tf.argmax(logits,1), tf.argmax(y_,1))
accuracy = tf.reduce_mean(tf.cast(correct_prediction, tf.float32))

# Build graph
init = tf.global_variables_initializer()

# Avoid allocating the whole memory
gpu_options = tf.GPUOptions(per_process_gpu_memory_fraction=0.333)
sess = tf.Session(config=tf.ConfigProto(gpu_options=gpu_options))
sess.run(init)

# Train graph
for i in range(2000):
    # Get batch of 50 images
    batch = mnist.train.next_batch(50)

    # Print each 100 epochs
    if i % 100 == 0:
        # Calculate train accuracy
        train_accuracy = accuracy.eval(session=sess, feed_dict={x_:
batch[0], y_: batch[1], is_training: True})
        print("step %d, training accuracy %g" % (i, train_accuracy))

    # Train actually here
    train_step.run(session=sess, feed_dict={x_: batch[0], y_: batch[1],
is_training: False})

print("Test Accuracy:",sess.run(accuracy, feed_dict={x_: mnist.test.images,
y_: mnist.test.labels, is_training: False}))
```

TensorBoard

TensorBoard is a web-based utility provided with TensorFlow that allows you to visualize your constructed TensorFlow graph. On top of this, it allows you to keep track of a wealth of statistics or variables that may be important for training your model. The examples of such variables that you might like to keep track of include training loss, test set accuracy, or learning rate. We saw earlier that we can visualize the value of our loss function using tensorboard.

To run TensorBoard, open a new terminal and type the following:

```
$ tensorboard --logdir=/somepath
```

Here, `somepath` points to the place where your training code saves tensorboard logging data.

Inside your code, you need to define which tensors to visualize by creating a `tf.summary` for each one. So for example if we wanted to to inspect all trainable variables and the loss we would need to use the following code:

```
with tf.Session() as sess:

    """Create your model"""

    # Add all trainable variables to tensorboard
    for var in tf.trainable_variables():
        tf.summary.histogram(var.name, var)
    # Add loss to tensorboard
    tf.summary.scalar("softmax_cross_entropy", loss)
    # Merge all summaries
    merged_summary = tf.summary.merge_all()
    # Initialize a summary writer
    train_writer = tf.summary.FileWriter( /tmp/summarys/ , sess.graph)

    train_writer.add_summary(merged_summary, global_step)

    """Training loop"""
```

We need to create a `tf.summar.FileWriter` which is responsible for creating a directory where logs of our summaries will be stored. If we pass in a graph when we create the FileWriter then this will also be displayed in TensorBoard for us. By passing in sess.graph we are supplying the default graph that the session is using. The result of displaying a graph in TensorBoard might look something like this:

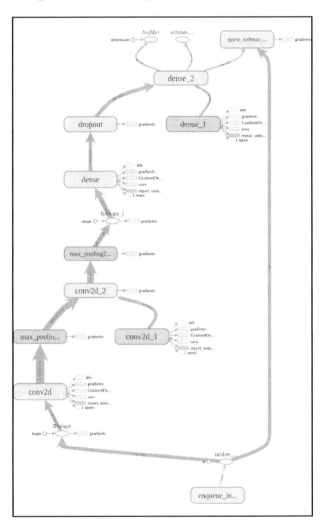

Other types of convolutions

The idea of this chapter was to give you a taste of what CNNs are, what they are used for, and how to construct them in TensorFlow. However, it is useful to mention at this point that there are other types of convolution operations used nowadays for different purposes, and we will look at some of them in more detail in later chapters.

For now, we will just mention them by name and where they are used:

- **Depthwise convolution**: Used in MobileNets, they aim to make convolutions friendly for mobile platforms
- **Dilated convolutions (Atrous convolution)**: They have an extra parameter called dilation rate that allows you to have a bigger field of view with the same computation cost (for instance, a 3x3 CONV could have the same field of view as a 5x5 CONV)
- **Transposed convolutions (Deconvolutions)**: Used normally in CNN autoencoders and in semantic segmentation problems

Summary

In this chapter, we introduced you to ML and artificial intelligence. We looked at what artificial neural networks are and how to train them. After this, we looked at CNNs and their main building blocks. We explained how to use TensorFlow to train your own CNN for recognizing digits. Finally, we had an introduction to Tensorboard and saw how it can be used to help visualize important statistics while training models in TensorFlow.

In the next chapter, we are going to look more closely at the task of image classification and how we can use CNNs and TensorFlow to solve this task.

Image Classification in TensorFlow

3

Image classification refers to the problem of classifying images into categories according to their contents. Let's start with an example task of classifying, where a picture may be an image of a dog, or not. A naive approach that someone might take to accomplish this task is to take an input image, reshape it into a vector, and then train a linear classifier (or some other kind of classifier), like we did in Chapter 1, Setup and Introduction to TensorFlow. However, you would very quickly discover that this idea is bad for several reasons. Besides not scaling well to the size of your input image, your linear classifier will simply have a hard time being able to separate one image from another.

In contrast to humans, who can see meaningful patterns and content in an image, the computer only sees an array of numbers from 0 to 255. The wide fluctuation of these numbers at the same locations for different images of the same class prohibits using them directly as an input to the classifier. These 10 example dog images taken from **Canadian Institute For Advanced Research (CIFAR)** dataset illustrate this problem perfectly. Not only does the appearance of dogs differ, but their pose and position in front of the camera also does. For a machine, each image at a glance is completely different with no commonalities, whereas we as humans can clearly see that these are all dogs:

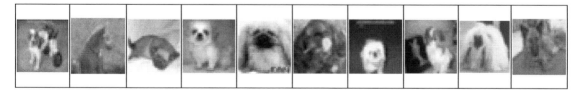

A better solution to our problem might be to tell the computer to extract some meaningful features from an input image, for example, common shapes, textures, or colors. We could then use these features, rather than the raw input image, as input to our classifier. Now, we are looking for the presence of these features in an image to tell us if it contains the object we want to identify or not.

These extracted features will look to us as simply a high-dimensional vector (but usually a much lower dimension than the original image space) that can be used as input for our classifier. Some well-known feature extraction methods that have been developed over the years are **scale invariant features (SIFT)**, **maximally stable extremal regions (MSER)**, **local binary patterns (LBP)**, and **histogram of oriented gradients (HOG)**.

The year 2012 saw one of the biggest turning points for Computer Vision (and subsequently, other machine learning areas) when the use of convolutional neural networks for image classification started a paradigm shift in how to solve this task (and many others). Rather than focusing on handcrafting better features to extract from our images, we use a data-driven approach that finds the optimal set of features to represent our problem dataset. A CNN will use large number of training images and learn for itself the best features to represent our data in order to solve the classification task.

In this chapter, we will cover the following topics:

- A look at the loss functions used for classification
- The Imagenet and CIFAR datasets
- Training a CNN to classify the CIFAR dataset
- Introduction to the data API
- How to initialize your weights
- How to regularize your models to get better results

CNN model architecture

The crucial part of an image classification model is its CNN layers. These layers will be responsible for extracting features from image data. The output of these CNN layers will be a feature vector, which like before, we can use as input for the classifier of our choice. For many CNN models, the classifier will be just a fully connected layer attached to the output of our CNN. As shown in `Chapter 1`, *Setup and Introduction to TensorFlow*, our linear classifier is just a fully connected layer; this is exactly the case here, except that the size and input to the layer will be different.

It is important to note that at its core, the CNN architecture used in classification or a regression problem such as localization (or any other problems that use images for that matter) would be the same. The only real difference will be what happens after the CNN layers have done their feature extraction. For example, one difference could be the loss function used for different tasks, as it is shown in the following diagram:

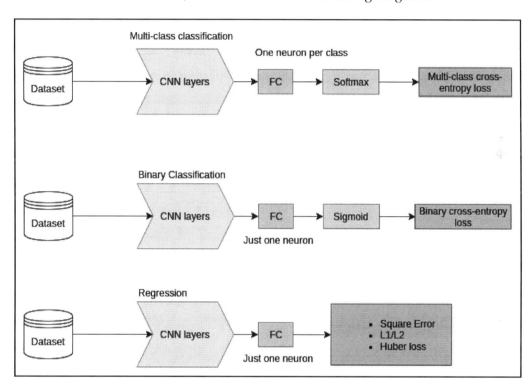

You will see a recurring pattern in this book when we look at the different problems that CNNs can be used to solve. It will become apparent that lots of tasks involving images can be solved using a CNN to extract some meaningful feature vector from the input data, which will then be manipulated in some way and fed to different loss functions, depending on the task. For now, let's crack on and focus firstly on the task of image classification by looking at the loss functions commonly used for it.

Cross-entropy loss (log loss)

The simplest form of image classification is binary classification. This is where we have a classifier that has just one object to classify, for example, dog/no dog. In this case, a loss function we are likely to use is the binary cross-entropy loss.

The cross entropy function between true labels p and model predictions q is defined as:

$$H(p, q) = -\sum_i p_i \log(q_i)$$

With i being the index for each possible element of our labels and predictions.

However, as we are dealing with the binary case when we have only two possible outcomes, y=1 and y=0, then $p \in \{y, 1 - y\}$ and $q \in \{\hat{y}, 1 - \hat{y}\}$ can be simplified down and we get:

$$H(p, q) = -(y\log(\hat{y}) + (1 - y)\log(1 - \hat{y}))$$

This is equivalent

Iterating over m training examples, the cost function L to be minimized then becomes this:

$$L(\hat{y}, y) = -\frac{1}{m}\sum_{i=1}^{m}(y_i \log(\hat{y}_i) + (1 - y_i)\log(1 - \hat{y}_i))$$

This is intuitively correct, as when $y = 1$, we want to minimize $L(\hat{y}, y) = -\log\hat{y}$, which requires large $\hat{y}$ and when $y = 0$, we want to minimize $L(\hat{y}, y) = -\log(1 - \hat{y})$, which requires a small $\hat{y}$.

In TensorFlow, the binary cross entropy loss can be found in the `tf.losses` module. It is useful to know that the name for the raw output $\hat{y}$ of our model is logits. Before we can pass this to the cross entropy loss we need to apply the **sigmoid** function to it so our output is scaled between 0 and 1. TensorFlow actually combines all these steps together into one operation, as shown in the code below. Also TensorFlow will take care of averaging the loss across the batch for us.

```
loss = tf.losses.sigmoid_cross_entropy(multi_class_labels=labels_in,
logits=model_prediction)
```

Multi-class cross entropy loss

Multi-class cross entropy loss is used in multi-class classification, such as the MNIST digits classification problem from Chapter 2, *Deep Learning and Convolutional Neural Networks*. Like above we use the cross entropy function which after a few calculations we obtain the multi-class cross-entropy loss L for each training example being:

$$L(\hat{y}, y) = -\sum_{k}^{K} y^{(k)} \log \hat{y}^{(k)}$$

Here, $y^{(k)}$ is 0 or 1, indicating whether class label k is the correct classification for predicting $\hat{y}^{(k)}$. To use this loss, we first need to add a softmax activation to the output $\hat{y}$ of the final FC layer in our model. The combined cross-entropy with softmax looks like this:

$$L(\hat{y}, y) = -\sum_{k}^{K} y^{(k)} \log \frac{e^{\hat{y}^{(k)}}}{\sum_{j=1}^{K} e^{\hat{y}^{(j)}}}$$

It is useful to know that the name for the raw output $\hat{y}$ of our model is logits. Logits are what is passed to the softmax function. The softmax function is the multi-class version of the sigmoid function. Once it is passed through the softmax function, we can use our multi-class cross entropy loss. TensorFlow actually combines all these steps together into one operation, as shown:

```
loss =
tf.reduce_mean(tf.nn.softmax_cross_entropy_with_logits(logits=model_logits,
labels=labels_in))
```

We must use tf.reduce_mean, as we will get a loss value for each image in our batch. We use tf.reduce_mean to get the average loss for our batch.

We could have used the tf.losses module again, specifically tf.losses.softmax_cross_entropy, similar to above and then we wouldn't need the tf.reduce_mean but we decided to show you a different way just so you can see there is many ways to do the same thing in TensorFlow. As TensorFlow has grown so has the number of different ways of achieving the same outcome and no way is usually much worse than others.

The train/test dataset split

For the time being, be aware that we need to split our dataset into two sets: training and test. As mentioned in `Chapter 1`, *Setup and Introduction to TensorFlow*, this needs to be done because we need to somehow check whether the model is able to generalize out of its own training samples (whether it's able to correctly recognize images that it has never seen during training). If our model can't do this, it isn't of much use to us.

Here are a few other important points to remember:

- The training and testing data must come from the same distribution (so combine and shuffle all your data before splitting)
- The training set is often bigger than the test set (for instance, training: 70% of total, testing: 30% of total).

For the examples that we will deal with in these early chapters, these basics will be enough, but in subsequent chapters, we will see, in further detail, how to properly set up your dataset for bigger projects.

Datasets

In this section, we will discuss the most important and famous recent datasets used in image classification. This is necessary, because it is likely that any perusal into Computer Vision will overlap with them (including in this book!). Before the arrival of convolutional neural networks, the two main datasets used in image classification competitions by the research community were the Caltech and PASCAL datasets.

The Caltech dataset was established by California Institute of Technology and was released in two versions. Caltech-101 was published in 2003 with 101 categories of about 40 to 800 images per category, and Caltech-256 in 2007 with 256 object categories, containing a total of 30607 images. The images were collected from Google images and PicSearch, and their size was roughly 300x400 pixels.

The Pascal **Visual Object Classes** (**VOC**) challenge was established in 2005. Organized every year till 2012, it provides a famous benchmark dataset of a wide range of natural images for *Image category Classification, Object detection, Segmentation, and Action Classification*. It is a diverse dataset that includes images from flickr of various sizes, pose, orientation, illumination, and occlusion. It has been developed in stages from the year 2005 (only four classes: bicycles, cars, motorbikes, and people, train/validation/test: 1578 images containing 2209 annotated objects) to year 2012 (twenty classes, The train/validation data has 11,530 images containing 27,450 ROI annotated objects and 6,929 segmentations).

The major change came with the PASCAL (VOC) 2007 challenge, when the number of classes increased from 4 to 20 and have been fixed since then. Evaluation metrics for the Classification task changed to average precision. The annotation for test data are only provided until the VOC 2007 challenge.

With the arrival of more sophisticated classification methods, the preceding datasets were not sufficient, and the ImageNet dataset along with the CIFAR dataset, described in the following sections, became the new standards in classification testing.

ImageNet

The ImageNet dataset was created in 2010 as a collaborative effort of Alex Berg (Columbia University), Jia Deng (Princeton University), and Fei-Fei Li (Stanford University) to run as a tester competition on large-scale visual recognition, in conjunction with the *PASCAL Visual Object Classes Challenge*, 2010. The dataset is a collection of images that represent the contents of WordNet. WordNet is a lexical database for the English language. It groups English words into sets of synonyms called **synsets** in a hierarchical structure. The following screenshot shows the WordNet structure of nouns. The number in the brackets is the number of synsets in the subtree.

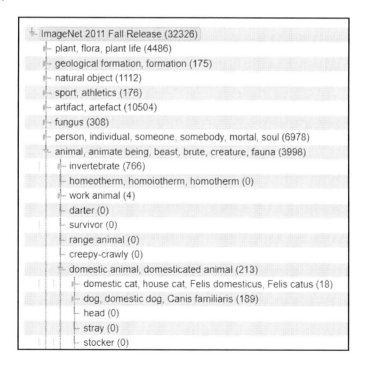

The evolution of image classification algorithms, which almost solved the classification challenge on the existing datasets led to the need for a new dataset that would allow image classification at a large scale. This is closer to a real-world scenario where we would like the machine to describe the content of an arbitrary image simulating human capability. Compared to its predecessors, where the number of classes is in the 100s, ImageNet offers over 10 million high-quality images covering more than 10,000 classes. Many of these classes are related to each other, which makes the task of classification more challenging, for example, distinguishing many breeds of dogs. Since the dataset is enormously huge, it was hard to annotate each image with all the classes that are present in it, so by convention, each image was labeled only with one class.

Since 2010, the annual ImageNet Large Scale Visual Recognition Challenge (ILSVRC) challenge focuses on image classification, single-object localization, and detection. The data for the object classification challenge consists of 1.2 million images (from 1000 categories/synsets), of training data, 50,000 images of validation data, and 100,000 images of testing data.

In the classification challenge the main metric used to evaluate an algorithm is the top-5 error rate. The algorithm is allowed to give five predicted classes and will not be penalized if at least one of the predicted classes matches the ground truth label.

Formally if we let i be the image and C_i be the ground truth label. Then, we have the predicted labels $c_{ij}, j \in [1,5]$, where at least one is equal to C_i to consider it a successful prediction. Consider that the error of a prediction is as follows:

$$d_{ij} = \begin{cases} 0 & c_{ij} = C_i \\ 1 & c_{ij} \neq C_i \end{cases}$$

Meaning the final error of an algorithm is then the proportion of test images on which a mistake was made, as shown:

$$error = \frac{1}{N} \sum_{i=1}^{N} \min_{j} d_{ij}$$

Imagenet was one of the big reasons why deep learning has taken off in recent years. Before deep learning became popular the top-5 error rate in ILSVRC was around 28% and not going down much at all. However, in 2012, the winner of the challenge, SuperVision, smashed the top-5 classification error down to 16.4%. The teams model, now known as AlexNet, was a deep convolutional neural network. This huge victory woke people up to the power of CNNs and it became the stepping stone for many modern CNN architectures.

In the following years CNN models continued to dominate and the top-5 error rate kept falling. The 2014 winner GoogLeNet reduced the error rate to 6.7% and this was halved again in 2015 to 3.57% by ResNet. Since then there has been smaller improvements with 2017's winner "WMW squeeze and excitation networks" produced a 2.25% error.

CIFAR

The CIFAR-10 and CIFAR-100 datasets are small (compared to modern standards) image datasets collected by Alex Krizhevsky, Vinod Nair, and Geoffrey Hinton. These datasets are widely used by the research community for image classification tasks. They are considered challenging, because the image quality is very low and the objects in the images are sometimes partially visible. At the same time, the datasets are convenient due to this small image size, so researchers can quickly produce results on them. CIFAR-100 increases the challenge since there are only a small number of images per class and the number of classes is fairly large. The CIFAR10 and CIFAR100 datasets contain 60,000 images each. Images in both datasets are 32x32x3 RGB color images.

In CIFAR-10, there are 10 classes and each class has 6,000 images. The dataset is divided into 50,000 training images and 10,000 test images. The following is the list of classes and some random images from each class from the CIFAR-10 dataset, so you can see what it looks like:

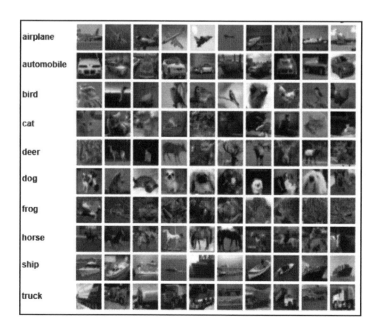

CIFAR-100 has 100 classes and 600 images per class. These 100 classes are divided into 20 superclasses. Each image has a **fine** label (the class that it belongs to) and a **coarse** label (the superclass it belongs to). The list of classes and Superclasses in CIFAR-100 is available at `https://www.cs.toronto.edu/~kriz/cifar.html`. Increasing the number of classes from coarse (20) to fine (100) can be helpful to maximize inter-class variability. This means that we want our model to consider two similar-looking objects in the image to belong to a different class. For example, a bed and a couch look similar but not exactly the same, and placing them in separate classes will ensure that they look different to the trained models.

The algorithm evaluation process for CIFAR is the same as in ImageNet. The best reported top-1 error for CIFAR-10 is 3.58%, and for CIFAR-100 is 17.31%, as reported by Saining Xie et al. in *Aggregated Residual Transformations for Deep Neural Networks*, where they presented the novel ResNeXt architecture. The Current state-of-the-art techniques for image classification using *Deep learning results on CIFAR-10 and CIFAR-100* can be found at `http://rodrigob.github.io/are_we_there_yet/build/classification_datasets_results.html` and `https://github.com/RedditSota/state-of-the-art-result-for-machine-learning-problems`.

Loading CIFAR

The datasets can be downloaded from the official website mentioned previously in Python, Matlab, and binary versions. There are different ways to load and read these datasets. In practice, within our TensorFlow implementations, we load it using the Keras library (`https://keras.io/`), which is now a part of TensorFlow in the `tf.keras` module. Here, we present some example code to load the CIFAR-10 dataset, but the CIFAR-100 dataset could be loaded in much the same way:

```
import tensorflow as tf

from tf.keras.datasets import cifar10


(x_train, y_train), (x_test, y_test) = cifar10.load_data()

print('x_train shape:',x_train.shape)

print('y_train shape:',y_train.shape)

print('x_test shape:',x_test.shape)

print('y_test shape:',y_test.shape)
```

```
print('x_train.shape[0]:',training samples)

print('x_test.shape[0]:',test samples)


# Convert class vectors to binary class matrices

y_train = tf.keras.utils.to_categorical(y_train,10)

y_test = tf.keras.utils.to_categorical(y_test,10)
```

This code returns two tuples:

```
x_train, x_test: uint8 array of RGB image data with shape (num_samples, 3,
32, 32)
y_train, y_test: uint8 array of category labels (integers in range 0-9)
with shape (num_samples,)
```

Output from the preceding code's print statements is as follows:

```
x_train shape:(50000,32,32,3

y_train shape:(50000,1)

x_test shape:(10000,32,32,3)

y_test shape:(10000,1)
```

Similarly, the CIFAR-100 dataset is loaded using the following:

```
from tf.keras.datasets import cifar100

 (x_train, y_train), (x_test, y_test) =
cifar100.load_data(label_mode='fine')
```

Image classification with TensorFlow

In this section, we will show you how to implement a relatively simple CNN architecture. We will also look at how to train it to classify the CIFAR-10 dataset.

Start by importing all the necessary libraries:

```
import fire
import numpy as np
import os
import tensorflow as tf
from tf.keras.datasets import cifar10
```

We will define a Python class that will implement the training process. The class name is Train, and it implements two methods: build_graph and train. The train function is fired when the main program is executed:

```
class Train:

    __x_ = []
    __y_ = []
    __logits = []
    __loss = []
    __train_step = []
    __merged_summary_op = []
    __saver = []
    __session = []
    __writer = []
    __is_training = []
    __loss_val = []
    __train_summary = []
    __val_summary = []



    def __init__(self):
        pass

    def build_graph(self):

    [...]

    def train(self, save_dir='./save', batch_size=500):

    [...]

if __name__ == '__main__':

    cnn= Train()

    cnn.train
```

Building the CNN graph

Let's go into detail through the `build_graph` function that contains the network definition, the loss function, and the optimizer used. First, we start the function by defining the placeholders for our inputs. We will use two placeholders to supply data and labels into the graph: `__x_` and `__y_`. The placeholder `__x_` will hold our input RGB images, while the placeholder `__y_` stores one hot labels of corresponding classes. We use `None` when defining the *N* part of the placeholder shape, as this tells TensorFlow that this value can be anything and will be supplied when we execute the graph:

```
def build_graph(self):
        self.__x_ = tf.placeholder("float", shape=[None, 32, 32, 3],
name='X')

        self.__y_ = tf.placeholder("int32", shape=[None, 10], name='Y')

        self.__is_training = tf.placeholder(tf.bool)
```

Then, we will define our network within the `name_scope` model. `Name_scope` returns a context manager for use when defining TensorFlow ops. This context manager validates that the variables are from the same graph, makes that graph the default graph, and pushes a name scope in that graph.

For this model, we will construct a simple CNN with three convolutional layers, three pooling layers, and two fully connected layers. We use the `tf.layers` API to construct the CNN layers. The `tf.reshape` function reshapes the tensor from the last pooling layer to a one-dimensional tensor to match what the dense layer expects to receive. The output of the final layer is assigned to `self.__logits`, which is the tensor that will be passed as input to our loss function:

```
        with tf.name_scope("model") as scope:

            conv1 = tf.layers.conv2d(inputs=self.__x_, filters=64,
kernel_size=[5, 5],

                                   padding="same", activation=tf.nn.relu)


            pool1 = tf.layers.max_pooling2d(inputs=conv1, pool_size=[2, 2],
strides=2)


            conv2 = tf.layers.conv2d(inputs=pool1, filters=64,
```

```
        kernel_size=[5, 5],

                                padding="same", activation=tf.nn.relu)


            pool2 = tf.layers.max_pooling2d(inputs=conv2, pool_size=[2, 2],
        strides=2)


            conv3 = tf.layers.conv2d(inputs=pool2, filters=32,
        kernel_size=[5, 5],

                                padding="same", activation=tf.nn.relu)


            pool3 = tf.layers.max_pooling2d(inputs=conv3, pool_size=[2, 2],
        strides=2)


            pool3_flat = tf.reshape(pool3,  [-1, 4 * 4 * 32])


            # FC layers
            FC1 = tf.layers.dense(inputs=pool3_flat, units=128,
        activation=tf.nn.relu)

            FC2 = tf.layers.dense(inputs=FC1, units=64,
        activation=tf.nn.relu)

            self.__logits = tf.layers.dense(inputs=FC2, units=10)
```

The next step is to define the loss function within the name scope `loss_func`. The loss function that is used here is the softmax cross entropy and, as mentioned earlier, we average the loss across the whole batch with `tf.reduce_mean`. We create variables to hold training `loss __loss` and validation loss `__loss_val`, and add these scalars to the TensorFlow summary data to display in TensorBoard later:

```
        with tf.name_scope("loss_func") as scope:

            self.__loss =
        tf.reduce_mean(tf.nn.softmax_cross_entropy_with_logits(logits=self.__logits
```

```
                    ,

labels=self.__y_))

                self.__loss_val =
tf.reduce_mean(tf.nn.softmax_cross_entropy_with_logits(logits=self.__logits
                    ,

labels=self.__y_))

                # Add loss to tensorboard

                self.__train_summary = tf.summary.scalar("loss_train",
self.__loss)

                self.__val_summary = tf.summary.scalar("loss_val",
self.__loss_val)
```

After defining our model and loss function, we need to specify which optimization function we will use to minimize the loss. The optimization function that we choose here is the Adam optimizer, and it is defined within the name scope *optimizer*.

Learning rate scheduling

In the last chapter, we briefly mentioned a problem that can occur by keeping a constant learning rate during training. As our model starts to learn, it is very likely that our initial learning rate will become too big for it to continue learning. The gradient descent updates will start overshooting or circling around our minimum; as a result, the loss function will not decrease in value. To solve this issue, we can, from time to time, decrease the value of the learning rate. This process is called learning rate scheduling, and there are several popular approaches.

The first method involves reducing the learning rate at fixed time steps during training, such as when training is 33% and 66% complete. Normally, you would decrease the learning rate by a factor of 10 when it reaches these set times.

The second approach involves reducing the learning rate according to an exponential or quadratic function of the time steps. An example of a function that would do this is as follows:

```
decayed_learning_rate = learning_rate * decay_rate ^ (global_step /
decay_steps)
```

By using this approach, the learning rate is smoothly decreased over the time of training.

A final approach is to use our validation set and look at the current accuracy on the validation set. While the validation accuracy keeps increasing, we do nothing to our learning rate. Once the validation accuracy stops increasing, we decrease the learning rate by some factor. This process is repeated until training finishes.

All methods can produce good results, and it may be worth trying out all these different methods when you train to see which one works better for you. For this particular model, we will use the second approach of an exponentially decaying learning rate. We use the TensorFlow operation—`tf.train.exponential_decay`—to do this, which follows the formula previously shown. As input, it takes the current learning rate, the global step, the amount of steps before decaying and a decay rate.

At every iteration, the current learning rate is supplied to our Adam Optimizer, which uses the `minimize` function that uses gradient descent to minimize the loss and increases the `global_step` variable by one. Lastly, `learning_rate` and `global_step` are added to the summary data to be displayed on TensorBoard during training:

```
with tf.name_scope("optimizer") as scope:
    global_step = tf.Variable(0, trainable=False)

    starter_learning_rate = 1e-3

    # decay every 10000 steps with a base of 0.96 function
    learning_rate =
tf.train.exponential_decay(starter_learning_rate, global_step,
                                              1000, 0.9,
staircase=True)
    self.__train_step =
tf.train.AdamOptimizer(learning_rate).minimize(self.__loss,
global_step=global_step)

    tf.summary.scalar("learning_rate", learning_rate)
    tf.summary.scalar("global_step", global_step)
```

Although the Adam optimizer automatically adjusts and decays the learning rate for us, we still find that having some form of learning rate scheduling as well improves results.

Once all the components of the graph have been defined, all the summaries collected in the graph are merged into `__merged_summary_op`, and all the variables of the graph are initialized by `tf.global_variables_initializer()`.

Naturally, while training the model, we want to store the network weights as binary files so that we can load them back to perform forward propagation. Those binary files in TensorFlow are called checkpoints, and they map variable names to tensor values. To save and restore variables to and from checkpoints, we use the `Saver` class. To avoid filling up disks, savers manage checkpoint files automatically. For example, they can keep only the *N* most recent files or one checkpoint for every *N* hours of training. In our case, we have set `max_to_keep` to `None`, which means all checkpoint files are kept:

```
# Merge op for tensorboard
self.__merged_summary_op = tf.summary.merge_all()

# Build graph
init = tf.global_variables_initializer()

# Saver for checkpoints
self.__saver = tf.train.Saver(max_to_keep=None)
```

In addition, we can specify the proportion of GPU memory to be used with `tf.GPUOptions`. The object session encapsulates the environment in which ops are executed and tensors are evaluated. After creating the `FileWriter` object to store the summaries and events to a file, the `__session.run(init)` method runs one step of TensorFlow computation, by running the necessary graph fragment to execute every operation and evaluate every tensor that was initialized in init as parts of the graph:

```
# Avoid allocating the whole memory

gpu_options = tf.GPUOptions(per_process_gpu_memory_fraction=0.6)

self.__session =
tf.Session(config=tf.ConfigProto(gpu_options=gpu_options))

# Configure summary to output at given directory

self.__writer = tf.summary.FileWriter("./logs/cifar10",
self.__session.graph)

self.__session.run(init)
```

Introduction to the tf.data API

Before continuing, we will take a look at TensorFlow's way of handling data input to any kind of model we might train. The TensorFlow `tf.data` API provides us with all the tools we might need to easily build complex input pipelines. One pipeline you might commonly build would involve loading raw training data, performing some preprocessing on it, shuffling, and then putting it into a batch ready for training. The `tf.data` API allows us to do all these steps in an easy way using simple and reusable pieces of code.

The `tf.data` API has two main components to it that you need to understand. The First is the `tf.data.Dataset`; this is what represents your raw data. More specifically, it holds a sequence of elements, where each element contains one or more tensor objects. For the task of image classification, one element would be a single training example, and it would consist of two tensors—one for the image and one for its corresponding label.

The second component is a `tf.data.Iterator`. These allow you to extract elements from your dataset and act as the connection between your dataset and your model code. There are several different types of iterators within TensorFlow that all serve different purposes and involve varying levels of difficulty to use.

Creating a dataset can be done in two ways. The first way is by creating a data source. An easy example is using `tf.data.Dataset.from_tensor_slices()`, which will create a dataset from slices of one or more Tensor objects. The other way of producing datasets is to use a dataset transformation on an existing dataset. Doing so will return a new dataset that incorporates the applied transformation. It's important to understand that all input pipelines must begin with a data source. Once you have a `Dataset` object, it is common to apply multiple transformations, all chained together, to it.

For now, some examples of simple transformations are `Dataset.batch()`, which will return batches of a set size from your `Dataset` object, and `Dataset.repeat()`, which will keep repeating the `Dataset` content when it reaches the end and is an easy way to be able to iterate over a dataset many times (count parameter).

Now that we have a dataset set up, we can use `tf.data.Iterators` to iterate over and extract elements from it. Again, there are several different kinds of iterators available to use, but the simplest one we will use is the one shot iterator. This iterator supports going through a dataset just once, but it's super simple to set up. We create it by calling the `make_one_shot_iterator()` method on our dataset and assigning the result to a variable. We can then call `get_next()` on our created iterator and assign it to another variable.

Now, whenever this op is run in a session, we will iterate once through the dataset, and a new batch will be extracted to use:

```
def train(self, save_dir='./save', batch_size=500):

    # Use keras to load the complete cifar dataset on memory (Not
scalable)

    (x_train, y_train), (x_test, y_test) = cifar10.load_data()


    # Convert class vectors to binary class matrices.

    y_train = tf.keras.utils.to_categorical(y_train, 10)

    y_test = tf.keras.utils.to_categorical(y_test, 10)



    # Using Tensorflow data Api to handle batches

    dataset_train = tf.data.Dataset.from_tensor_slices((x_train,
y_train))

    dataset_train = dataset_train.shuffle(buffer_size=10000)

    dataset_train = dataset_train.repeat()

    dataset_train = dataset_train.batch(batch_size)

    dataset_test = tf.data.Dataset.from_tensor_slices((x_test, y_test))

    dataset_test = dataset_test.repeat()

    dataset_test = dataset_test.batch(batch_size)



    # Create an iterator

    iter_train = dataset_train.make_one_shot_iterator()

    iter_train_op = iter_train.get_next()

    iter_test = dataset_test.make_one_shot_iterator()
```

```
iter_test_op = iter_test.get_next()



# Build model graph

self.build_graph()
```

The main training loop

Once we have retrieved the data and built the graph, we can start our main training loop, which will continue over 20,000 iterations. In every iteration, a batch of training data is taken using the CPU device, and the __train_step.run method of the AdamOptimizer object is called to run one forward and one backward pass. Every 100 iterations, we run a forward pass over the current training and testing batch to collect training and validation loss, and other summary data. Then, the add_summary method of the FileWriter object wraps the provided TensorFlow summaries: summary_1 and summary_2 in an event protocol buffer and adds it to the event file:

```
# Train Loop
for i in range(20000):


    batch_train = self.__session.run([iter_train_op])
    batch_x_train, batch_y_train = batch_train[0]

    # Print loss from time to time
    if i % 100 == 0:

        batch_test = self.__session.run([iter_test_op])
        batch_x_test, batch_y_test = batch_test[0]



        loss_train, summary_1 = self.__session.run([self.__loss,
self.__merged_summary_op],

                                        feed_dict={self.__x:
batch_x_train,

                                        self.__y_:
batch_y_train,
self.__is_training: True})
```

```
        loss_val, summary_2 = self.__session.run([self.__loss_val,
self.__val_summary],

feed_dict={self.__x_: batch_x_test,

self.__y_: batch_y_test,
self.__is_training: False})

            print("Loss Train: {0} Loss Val: {1}".format(loss_train,
loss_val))

            # Write to tensorboard summary
            self.__writer.add_summary(summary_1, i)
            self.__writer.add_summary(summary_2, i)



        # Execute train op
        self.__train_step.run(session=self.__session, feed_dict={
            self.__x_: batch_x_train, self.__y_: batch_y_train,
self.__is_training: True})
```

Once the training loop is over, we store the final model into a checkpoint file with `op`
`__saver.save`:

```
    # Save model
    if not os.path.exists(save_dir):
        os.makedirs(save_dir)

    checkpoint_path = os.path.join(save_dir, "model")
    filename = self.__saver.save(self.__session, checkpoint_path)
    print("Model saved in file: %s" % filename)
```

Model Initialization

As we add more and more layers to our models, it becomes harder and harder to train them
using backpropagation. The error values that are passed back through the model to update
weights become smaller and smaller the deeper we go. This is known as the vanishing
gradient problem.

As a result, an important thing to look at before we start training our models is what values we initialize our weights to. A bad initialization can make the model very slow to converge, or perhaps never converge at all.

Although we do not know exactly what values our weights will end up with after training, one might reasonably expect that about half of them will be positive values and half will be negative.

Do not initialize all weights with zeros

We might be inclined to now think that setting all our weights to zero will achieve maximum symmetry. However, this is actually a very bad idea, and our model will never learn anything. This is because when you do a forward pass, every neuron will produce the same result; so, during the backpropagation step, all the weights will update in the same way. This means the model can never learn an informative set of features, so don't initialize like this.

Initializing with a mean zero distribution

A better idea is to initialize your weights with small random values all centered at zero. For this, we can use random values from a normal distribution with zero mean and unit variance, which are then scaled by some small value, such as 0.01.

Doing this will break the symmetry in the weights as they will all be random and unique, which is a good thing. Calculating the forward and backward passes, our model neurons will now update in distinct ways. This will give them the chance to learn many different features that will all work together as part of a big neural network.

The only thing to then worry about is how small we set our weight values. If set too small, backpropagation updates will also be very small, which can cause vanishing gradient problems in deeper networks.

The following illustration shows one of the requirements for the weights (Zero-mean):

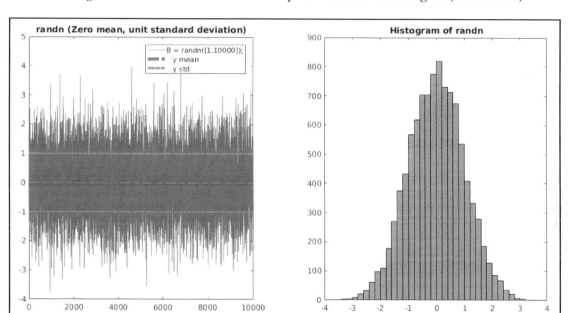

Xavier-Bengio and the Initializer

In their paper, *Understanding the difficulty of training deep feedforward neural networks*, Xavier Glorot and Yoshua Bengio showed that if the weights at each layer are initialized from a uniform distribution $U[-1/\sqrt{n}, 1/\sqrt{n}]$, where n is the size of the previous layer, then for sigmoid activation function, the neurons of the top layers (closer to the output) quickly saturate to 0. We understand that due to the form of the sigmoid function, an activation value of 0 means very large weights and a backpropagated gradient approaching to zero. Extremely small gradient values slow down the learning process as the weights in earlier layers stop being updated or otherwise stop learning.

Therefore, what we want is to keep our weights uniformly distributed within the initially decided interval, that is, the variance of weights should remain unchanged as we travel from the bottom to top layers. This will allow the error to flow smoothly to the top layers and consequently, the network to converge faster during training.

In order to achieve that, Glorot and Bengio prove that for a symmetric activation function f with unit derivative at 0, the variance of weights at each layer must be as follows:

$$Var[W^l] = \frac{2}{n_{out} + n_{in}}$$

Here, n_{in} is the number of units to the layer under question, and n_{out} is the number of units at the following layer. This means that the weights must be sampled from the following uniform distribution:

$$W \sim U \left[-\sqrt{\frac{6}{n_{out} + n_{in}}}, \sqrt{\frac{6}{n_{out} + n_{in}}} \right]$$

We can also sample the weights from a normal distribution with zero mean and the preceding variance.

For a ReLu activation function, it is proven by He et al. that the variances should instead be

$$Var[W^l] = \frac{2}{n_{in}}.$$

Hence, the authors initialize their weights with a zero-mean Gaussian distribution, whose standard deviation (std) is $\sqrt{2/n_{in}}$. This initialization is then called He initialization.

By default, TensorFlow uses the Glorot (xavier) initializer for most of its `tf.layers`, but we can override this and specify our own initialization. Here, we show an example of how to override the default initializer of the `conv2d` layer:

```
conv1 = tf.layers.conv2d(inputs=self.__x_, filters=64, kernel_size=[5, 5],

                padding="same", activation=None,

kernel_initializer=tf.truncated_normal_initializer(stddev=0.01),

bias_initializer=tf.zeros_initializer())
```

Improving generalization by regularizing

So far in this chapter, we have seen how we would use TensorFlow to train a convolutional neural network for the task of image classification. After we trained our model, we ran it through the test set, which was stored away at the start, to see how well it would perform on data it had never seen before. This process of evaluating our model on a test set gives us an indication of how well our model will generalize when we deploy it. A model that generalizes well is clearly a desirable property to have, as it allows it to be used in many situations.

What CNN architecture we use is one of the ways that we can improve the generalization ability of our model. One simple technique to keep in mind is to start by designing your model as simply as possible with few layers or filters. Since very small models are more likely to underfit to your data, you can slowly add complexity until underfitting stops occurring. If you design your models this way, it limits the possibility that overfitting ever occurs, as you don't allow yourself to have a model that is too large for your dataset.

In this section, however, we will explore some of the other things we can do to make a better machine learning model and how to incorporate them into our training procedure. The following methods aim to prevent overfitting and by doing so, help create a more robust model that generalizes better. The process of preventing our model from overfitting is called **regularization**.

Another problem that could also occur and can look very similar to overfitting is if your training dataset does not capture the whole variety of things that you want to classify. If you were, for example, training a dog classifier but your training images only contain images of Poodles. If you were to test this trained classifier on Labradors, it would likely fail to classify. This kind of data imbalance is a separate issue and will be addressed in the later chapters.

L2 and L1 regularization

The first way that we will look at to create a more robust model is to use L1 or L2 regularization. These are by far the most common methods of regularization. The basic idea is that during training of our model, we actively try to impose some constraint on the values of the model weights using either the L1 or L2 norms of those weights.

We do this by adding an extra term to whatever loss function we are using. For L1 regularization, the term we add is $\lambda \mid w \mid$, and for L2 regularization, the term we add is $0.5\lambda w^2$. In the preceding terms, w is all the weights in our network, and λ is a hyperparameter called the **regularization strength**. By adding this term, we prevent weight values from becoming too large.

Therefore, the SVM loss function, that is, $L = \frac{1}{N} \sum_{i=1}^{N} \sum_{j \neq y_i} \max(0, s_j - s_{y_i} + 1)$, from `Chapter` 1, *Setup and Introduction to TensorFlow*, for L1 regularization becomes as follows:

$$L = \frac{1}{N} \sum_{i=1}^{N} \sum_{j \neq y_i} \max(0, s_j - s_{y_i} + 1) + \lambda \sum_{l} \sum_{n} \sum_{m} | W_{m,n}^{l} |$$

Here, we add the regularization term that sums over all weights of the network. Here, l is the layer index, and m, n are the indexes of the weight matrix for each layer. The expression for L2 regularization will look similar.

For L1 regularization, this extra term encourages the weight vectors to become sparse, meaning that many of the weight values become zero. As a result, the model becomes immune to noisy inputs, as the weight vectors will only use a subset of the important inputs, which helps avoid overfitting.

For L2 regularization, this extra term, apart from keeping the sum of weights low, also forces the weight values to be evenly spread across the weight vectors so that the model uses all the weights a little bit rather than use a few weights a lot. Due to the multiplicative interaction between inputs and weights, this is intuitively a desirable property to have and helps the model avoid overfitting. L2 regularization is also sometimes called weight decay; this is because during training, all of your weights will be linearly reduced or 'decay' by the term (the derivative of the L2 regularization term).

Note that we do not include the bias term during regularization, only the weights. This is because the bias terms do not really affect a model's overfitting, as they affect the output in an additive way, just shifting up or down rather than changing the shape of your function. There is no harm to include them, but there's also no benefit, so consequently, there's no point in including them.

In the following diagram, you may note that increasing the regularization strength lambda reduces overfitting. A high regularization term means that the network becomes nearly linear and cannot shape complicated decision boundaries.

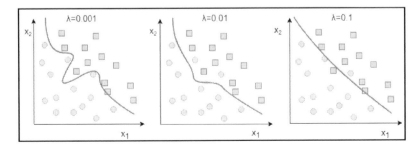

We can manually implement L2/L1 regularization by grabbing all our weights and applying the l2 norm to each, and then adding them all together, but this soon gets tedious for big models. Luckily, there is an easier way in TensorFlow if we are using `tf.layers`. First, we set up our regularizer, as demonstrated:

```
l2_reg = tf.contrib.layers.l2_regularizer(scale=0.001)
```

The scale argument is our lambda from before that we need to find and set ourselves, usually by cross validation. If we set it to 0, no regularization will occur. Now, when we create any layers, we pass our regularizer through as an argument. TensorFlow will do the calculations to get all the regularization terms we need to add to our loss function:

```
# Example of adding passing regularizer to a conv layer.
  reg_conv_layer = tf.layers.conv2d( inputs, filters, kernel_size,
kernel_regularizer=l2_reg)
```

To add our regularization terms, we first need to collect them all up. Luckily, TensorFlow will automatically place all of our regularization terms together in a collection for us, so that we can access them easily. TensorFlow stores some important collections associated with your created graph, such as trainable variables, summaries, and regularization losses, to name a few, inside `tf.GraphKeys`. We can access these collections using `tf.get_collection()` and supplying the name of a collection to get. For example, to get our regularization losses, we will write the following:

```
reg_losses = tf.get_collection(tf.GraphKeys.REGULARIZATION_LOSSES)
```

This will return a list containing all the tensors stored in this collection.

You can also make your own collections using `tf.get_collection(key='my_collection')` and then add variables to it using `tf.add_to_collection(name='my_collection', value=some_variable_to_add)`. If a collection already exists with the supplied key, `tf.get_collection` will return that collection rather than creating it.

Now that we have our regularization loss terms, we can just add them to our usual training loss, like so, and then optimize the combined loss:

```
train_loss=[...]  # Training loss

combined_loss = tf.n_add(train_loss, reg_losses)
```

Dropout

Another technique for regularization that we will look at is something called Dropout. Introduced in 2012 by G. E. Hinton, dropout is a simple method of regularization that gives very good results. The idea behind dropout is that at each training iteration, all the neurons in a layer may, with random probability (usually 50%), be turned on and off.

This turning on and off forces the network to learn the same concepts as usual, but via multiple different paths. After training, all neurons are kept on, and these paths will behave like an ensemble of multiple networks that will be used to average the final result, thus improving generalization. It forces the weight to be distributed across the whole network and keeps the low somewhat as regularization does.

Another way to understand the concept is by having a team where multiple people share similar knowledge; each one of them will have their own ideas on how to solve a particular problem, and an ensemble of those experiences provide a better way to solve the issue:

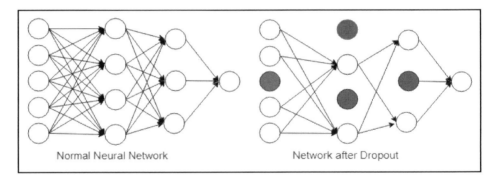

Normal Neural Network   Network after Dropout

In the following graph, we display the model test error. It's clear that with dropout, the error on the test set decreases. Remember that like with all regularization, using dropout will make your training loss increase compared to using no regularization, but at the end of the day, we're only interested in the model test error being lower (generalization):

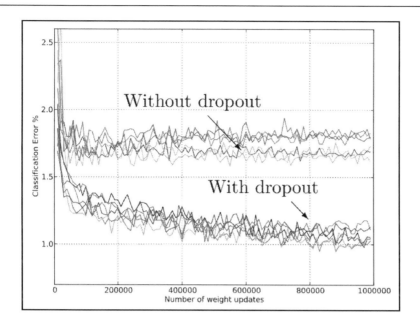

In general, dropout is applied only to the fully connected layers, but it can also be applied to convolutional/pooling layers; if this is done, you would use a lower *p* (probability of dropping out), something closer to 0.2. Also you place the dropout layer after the activation layer.

To use dropout in your TensorFlow model, we call `tf.layers.dropout()` on the input layer we wish to apply dropout to. We must also specify the dropout rate we want to use and, importantly, a Boolean letting TensorFlow know if our model is training or not. Remember that when we are using our model at test time, we turn dropout off, and this Boolean will do that for us. Hence, our code with dropout will look as follows:

```
# Fully connected layer (in tf contrib folder for now)

fc1 = tf.layers.dense(fc1, 1024)

# Apply Dropout (if is_training is False, dropout is not applied)

fc1 = tf.layers.dropout(fc1, rate=dropout, training=is_training)
```

The batch norm layer

Earlier, we took care of the initialization of our weights to make the job of gradient descent optimizers easier. However, the benefits are only seen during the early stages of training and do not guarantee improvements in the latter stages. That is where we turn to another great invention called the batch norm layer. The effect produced by using the batch norm layer in a CNN model is more or less the same as the input normalization that we saw in Chapter 2, *Deep Learning and Convolutional Neural Networks*; the only difference now is that this will happen at the output of all the convolution and fully connected layers in your model.

The batch norm layer will usually be attached to the end of every fully connected or convolution layer, but before the activation functions, where it will normalize the layer outputs, as it is shown in the following illustration. It does this by taking a layers output (a batch of activations) and subtracting the batch mean and dividing by the batch standard deviation, so the layer outputs have zero-mean and unit standard deviation. Be aware that the placement of batchnorm before or after activation functions is a hotly debated topic, but both should work.

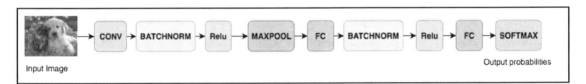

After this normalization, the batch norm layer also has two learnable parameters that will scale and shift the normalized activations to whatever the model thinks is best to help it learn. The whole process helps training by eliminating vanishing gradient problems. This, in turn, allows a model to use higher learning rates while training, so it converges in less iterations.

During training, a running average of mean and standard deviation values are recorded. These values are then used at test time rather than calculating batch statistics.

Some advantages of the batch norm layer are as follows:

- Improves gradient flow, allowing more deep networks to be trained (fixing the vanishing gradient issue)
- Allows higher learning rates, making the training faster
- Reduces the dependency on good weight initialization (simpler random initialization)

- Gives some sort of regularization effect to your model
- Makes it possible to use saturating nonlinearities such as sigmoid

For the more mathematical reader, a slightly more formal definition can be found in the batch norm paper "Batch Normalization: Accelerating Deep Network Training by Reducing Internal Covariate Shift", which is a really well-written paper that is easy to understand and explains the concept in much more detail. If we assume that we have a simple neural network with only fully connected layers, then as we saw in Chapter 1, *Setup and Introduction to TensorFlow*, an activation at each layer will be of the $s = f(x; W, b) = W \cdot x + b$ form.

Let's assume that $g(\cdot)$ is a nonlinearity, such as sigmoid or ReLU, then batch normalization $BN(\cdot)$ is applied to each unit directly before the nonlinearity as such:

$a = g(BN(W \cdot x + b))$

Here, the bias can be ignored, as it will be canceled by mean subtraction. If our batch size is m then the normalized activation s_i^{BN} is calculated as follows:

$$\mu_B = \frac{1}{m} \sum_{i=1}^{m} s_i$$

$$\sigma_B = \frac{1}{m} \sum_{i=1}^{m} (s_i - \mu_b)^2$$

$$\hat{s}_i = \frac{s_i - \mu_B}{\sqrt{\sigma^2 + \epsilon}}$$

$$s_i^{BN} = \gamma \hat{s}_i + \beta$$

where, γ and β are learnable parameters that will scale and shift your normalized activations. These parameters are there for the network to decide whether the normalization is needed or not, and how much. This is true, because if we set $\beta = \mu$ and $\gamma = \sqrt{\sigma^s + \epsilon}$, then $s_i^{BN} = s_i$.

Finally, here's an example of how to use the batch norm layer in the classification example code that we started in this chapter. In this case, we have put a batchnorm layer after a convolutional layer and before the activation function:

```
conv3 = tf.layers.conv2d(inputs=pool2, filters=32, kernel_size=[5,
```

```
5],padding="same", activation=None)
conv3_bn = tf.layers.batch_normalization(inputs=conv3, axis=-1,
momentum=0.9, epsilon=0.001, center=True,scale=True,
training=self.__is_training, name='conv3_bn')
conv3_bn_relu = tf.nn.relu(conv3_bn)
pool3 = tf.layers.max_pooling2d(inputs=conv3_bn_relu, pool_size=[2, 2],
strides=2)
```

Summary

In this chapter, we saw how CNN models are built, including what loss functions to use. We looked at the CIFAR and Imagenet datasets, and saw how to train a CNN for the task of classifying the CIFAR10 dataset. In doing so, we were introduced to the TensorFlow data API, which makes the task of loading and transforming data easier. Finally, we looked at ways to help improve the quality of our trained model by talking about different methods of initialization and regularization.

In the next chapter, we will solve the more difficult tasks of object detection, semantics, and instance segmentation.

4
Object Detection and Segmentation

From the previous chapter we know that Image classification only really deals with the case when we have a single instance of a class in an input image. Even then it only provides a coarse output for us, letting us know what object is present in an image but not where it is. A more interesting scenario is when we want to find where all instances of a class, or even multiple different classes, are located in an input image.

To deal with this more challenging problem, object detection and segmentation come into the picture. These are areas of computer vision that until recently were very challenging. However, applying convolutional neural networks to these problems has gained a lot of attention in recent years and consequently, for the most part, these problems can now be considered solved. In this chapter we will see how CNNs have managed to tackle these difficult tasks so well.

The following image shows the differences between different solutions Segmentation, Localization, Detection and Instance Segmentation:

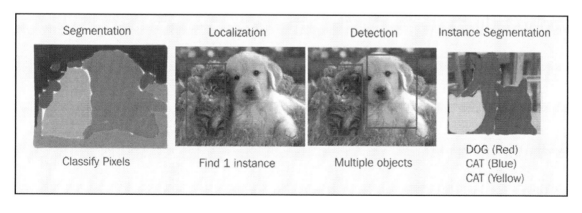

Before we start discussing object detection, we need to understand another important concept—localization. It is a key building block for improving classification and enabling detection. We will see that these three concepts are closely related to each other as we move from image classification to classification with localization, and finally to object detection.

In this chapter, we will learn about the following interesting topics:

- Image classification with localization
- Object detection
- Semantic segmentation
- Instance segmentation
- How to build convolutional neural networks to perform all these tasks

Image classification with localization

After learning about image classification in the last chapter, we now know that when we classify an image, we are just trying to output the class label of an object inside that image. Usually, to make the task easier, there will be only one object in the image.

Moving forward, in many cases, we are also interested in finding the location of an object in the image. The name given to this task of locating an object is called **localization**. In this case, the output we want to produce is the coordinates of a box that goes around the object. The name for this box is the bounding box or bounding rectangle. The important detail about localization is that we only localize one object per image.

When we build a model responsible for predicting a class label as well as the bounding box around the object of interest, it is called **image classification with localization.**

Localization as regression

Localization can be achieved using a similar network architecture to the one we learned about in `Chapter 3`, *Image Classification in TensorFlow*.

In addition to predicting the class labels, we will output a flag indicating the presence of an object and also the coordinates of the object's bounding box. The bounding box coordinates are usually four numbers representing the upper-left x and y coordinates, along with the height and width of the box.

For example, in this case, we have two classes, C1 (Car) and C2 (People), to predict. The output of our network will look something like this:

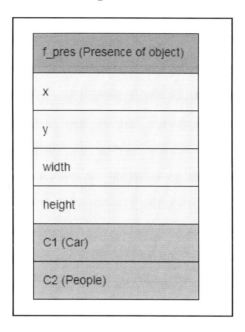

The model would work as follows:

1. We feed an input image to a CNN.
2. The CNN produces a feature vector that is fed to three different FC layers. Each of these different FC layers, or heads, will be responsible for predicting a different thing: Object presence, Object location, or Object class.
3. Three different losses are used in training: one for each head.
4. A ratio from the current training batch is calculated to weigh how much influence the classification and location loss will have, given the presence of objects. For example, if the batch has only 10% of images with objects, those losses will be multiplied by 0.1.

Just as a reminder: Outputting numbers (that is, 4 bounding box coordinates) is called **regression**.

Note that important distinction between classification and regression is that with classification, we get discrete/categorical outputs, whereas regression provides continuous values as output. We present the model in diagram as follows:

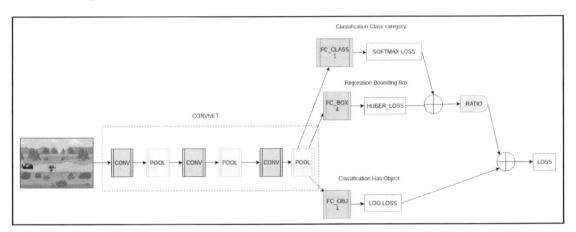

From the diagram, we can clearly see the three heads of fully-connected layers, each outputting a different loss (presence, class, and box). The losses used are logistic regression/log loss, cross entropy/softmax loss, and Huber loss. Huber loss is a loss we haven't seen before; it is a loss used for regression that is a sort of combination of the L1 and L2 losses.

The regression loss for localization gives some measure of dissimilarity between the ground-truth bounding-box coordinates of the object in the image and the bounding-box coordinates that the model predicts. We use the Huber loss here, but various different loss functions could be used instead, such as L2, L1, or smooth L1 loss.

The classification loss and localization loss are combined and weighted by a scalar ratio. The idea here is that we are only interested in backpropagating the classification and bounding-box losses if there is an object there in the first place.

The complete loss formula for this model is as follows:

$$Loss_{loc} = Log_{loss}{}^{presence} + ratio * (Softmax_{loss}{}^{class} + Huber_{loss}{}^{box})$$

TensorFlow implementation

Now, we will present how this kind of model might be implemented in TensorFlow. It is extremely similar to a model for classification, except that we have multiple output layers at the end instead of just one, and each has its own loss function:

```python
def build_graph(self):
    self.__x_ = tf.placeholder("float", shape=[None, 240, 320, 3], name='X')
    self.__y_box = tf.placeholder("float", shape=[None, 4], name='Y_box')
    self.__y_obj = tf.placeholder("float", shape=[None, 1], name='Y_obj')
    # Training flag for dropout in the fully connected layers
    self.__is_training = tf.placeholder(tf.bool)

    with tf.name_scope("model") as scope:
        conv1 = tf.layers.conv2d(inputs=self.__x_, filters=32,
kernel_size=[5, 5], padding="same", activation=tf.nn.relu)
        pool1 = tf.layers.max_pooling2d(inputs=conv1, pool_size=[2, 2],
strides=2)
        conv2 = tf.layers.conv2d(inputs=pool1, filters=64, kernel_size=[5,
5], padding="same", activation=tf.nn.relu)
        pool2 = tf.layers.max_pooling2d(inputs=conv2, pool_size=[2, 2],
strides=2)
        conv3 = tf.layers.conv2d(inputs=pool2, filters=32, kernel_size=[5,
5], padding="same", activation=tf.nn.relu)
        pool3 = tf.layers.max_pooling2d(inputs=conv3, pool_size=[2, 2],
strides=2)
        pool3_flat = tf.reshape(pool3, [-1, 40 * 30 * 32])

        # 2 Head version (has object head, and bounding box)
        self.__model_box = tf.layers.dense(inputs=pool3_flat, units=4)
        self.__model_has_obj = tf.layers.dense(inputs=pool3_flat, units=1,
activation=tf.nn.sigmoid)

    with tf.name_scope("loss_func") as scope:
        loss_obj = tf.losses.log_loss(labels=self.__y_obj,
predictions=self.__model_has_obj)
        loss_bbox = tf.losses.huber_loss(labels=self.__y_box,
predictions=self.__model_box)
        # Get ratio of samples with objects
        batch_size = tf.cast(tf.shape(self.__y_obj)[0], tf.float32)
        num_objects_label = tf.cast(tf.count_nonzero(tf.cast(self.__y_obj >
0.0, tf.float32)), tf.float32)
        ratio_has_objects = (num_objects_label * tf.constant(100.0)) /
batch_size
        # Loss function that has an "ignore" factor on the bbox loss when
objects is not detected
        self.__loss = loss_obj + (loss_bbox*ratio_has_objects)
```

```
        # Add loss to tensorboard
        tf.summary.scalar("loss", self.__loss)
        tf.summary.scalar("loss_bbox", loss_bbox)
        tf.summary.scalar("loss_obj", loss_obj)

    with tf.name_scope("optimizer") as scope:
        self.__train_step =
tf.train.AdamOptimizer(1e-4).minimize(self.__loss)

    # Merge op for tensorboard
    self.__merged_summary_op = tf.summary.merge_all()

    # Build graph
    init = tf.global_variables_initializer()

    # Saver for checkpoints
    self.__saver = tf.train.Saver(max_to_keep=None)

    # Avoid allocating the whole memory
    gpu_options = tf.GPUOptions(per_process_gpu_memory_fraction=0.6)
    self.__session =
tf.Session(config=tf.ConfigProto(gpu_options=gpu_options))
    # Configure summary to output at given directory
    self.__writer = tf.summary.FileWriter("./logs/loc_logs",
self.__session.graph)
    self.__session.run(init)
```

Other applications of localization

The idea of outputting the coordinates of points of interest in the image using CNNs can be extended to many other applications. Some of these include human-pose estimation (*DeepPose: Human Pose Estimation via Deep Neural Networks*), as shown:

The keypoints/landmarks are defined for the objects in the training images. These keypoint locations must be consistent for a particular object among all training images.

For example, in facial-keypoint detection, say we are interested in locating the eyes, nose, and mouth, we must define a number of key points around the eyes, nose, and mouth of all the training face images. We then train the CNN to output the predicted keypoint locations, just like in the preceding image, and then a regression loss is applied to these output key point coordinates to train the CNN. At test time, the input image is fed into CNN to predict all the keypoint positions. The following illustration shows facial-keypoint detection:

Object detection as classification – Sliding window

Object detection is a different problem to localization as we can have a variable number of objects in the image. Consequently it becomes very tricky to handle variable number of outputs if we consider detection as just a simple regression problem like we did for localization. Therefore we consider detection as a classification problem instead.

One very common approach that has been in use for a long time is to do object detection using sliding windows. The idea is to slide a window of fixed size across the input image. What is inside the window at each location is then sent to a classifier that will tell us if the window contains an object of interest or not.

For this purpose, one can first train a CNN classifier with small closely cropped images - resized to the same size as the window - of objects we want to detect e.g. cars. At test time our fixed size window is moved in a sliding fashion across the whole image that we want to detect objects in. Our CNN then predicts for each window if it is an object (a car in this case) or not.

With only one size of sliding window we can only detect one size of object. So, to find larger or smaller objects we can also use larger and smaller windows at test time and resize the contents before sending it to the classifier. Alternatively you can resize the whole input image and use only one size sliding window that will also run across these resized images. Both methods will work but the idea is to produce what is called a 'pyramid of scales' so we can detect different size objects in an image.

The big downfall of this method is there can be huge number of windows from various scales passing through the CNN for prediction. This makes it very computationally expensive to use with CNNs as the classifier. Also for the most of these windows they will contain no objects anyway.

Many improvements have been made to overcome this problem. In the following sections we will go through various techniques and algorithms that have been created to tackle the problem and how newer ones have improved on what came before them.

Using heuristics to guide us (R-CNN)

In order to avoid running a classifier at every possible position on the input image (when most won't contain an object), we can use some external method to propose likely regions to us. One method that can do this is called **Selective Search**.

The region-proposal method will provide blob-like rectangular regions in the image, which are likely to contain objects of interest. These regions are the candidate areas for the presence of an object of interest. A CNN classifier is then applied only on these proposed regions. This cuts down massively on the number of crops sent to the CNN for classification, as compared to the sliding window approach.

This particular approach was suggested in 2013 and was known as *R-CNN: Regions with CNN*. The following diagram depicts the process of R-CNN:

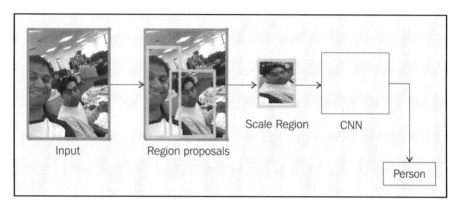

Problems

R-CNN is still computationally expensive, as you have to run a CNN on around 2,000 individual region proposals. As a result, it is very slow for both training and testing. The CNN classifier relies on the fixed number of rectangular candidate windows produced by selective search for detection. This method is not the fastest around and as proposal regions are not learned from the training data, they are probably not optimal for the task.

Fast R-CNN

In 2015, Fast R-CNN was proposed to remedy the speed problems of R-CNN. In this method, the main change is where we get proposal regions in the pipeline. Instead of getting them directly from the input image, we first run the entire input image through a CNN and extract the generated feature map close to the end of the network. Next, again using a region-proposal method, candidate regions are extracted from this feature map in a similar manner to R-CNN.

Getting proposals in this way helps reuse and share expensive convolutional computations. The fully connected layers further down in the network that will classify, and additionally localize, only accept fixed-size input. For this reason, the proposed regions from the feature map are warped to a fixed size using a new layer called **RoI pooling** (discussed further in the next section). RoI Pooling resizes the regions into the size needed by the last FC layers. The whole process is shown in the following diagram:

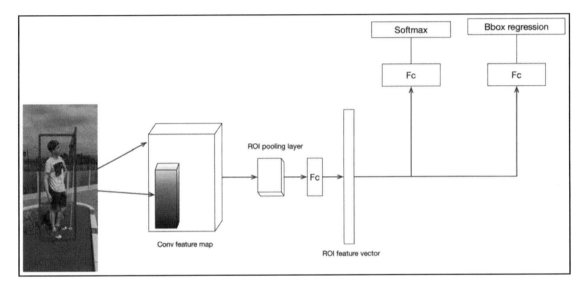

The comparison of R-CNN and FastRCNN shows that the latter is about 10 times faster at training time and nearly 150 times faster at test time (when using a VGG architecture as the main CNN).

Faster R-CNN

This technique, proposed shortly after Fast R-CNN in 2015, solves the need to use external region-proposal methods and removes the computational costs associated with them.

The main difference of this algorithm is that instead of using an external algorithm (such as selective search) for creating the proposals, a subnetwork called a **Region Proposal network (RPN)** is used to learn and generate proposals for us. This is shown in this screenshot:

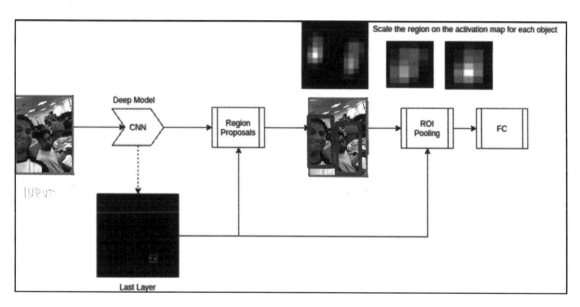

Region Proposal Network

The job of the RPN is to predict whether something we call an anchor (essentially just a bounding box) contains an object or is only background, and then to refine the position of this bounding box.

Basically, the RPN does this by sliding a small window (3 x 3) across the last CNN feature map (the same feature map Fast R-CNN gets proposals from). For every sliding window center, we create k fixed anchor boxes and classify those boxes as containing an object or not:

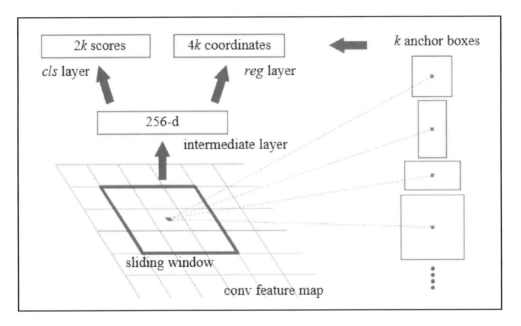

Internally, during training, we choose the anchor bounding box with the biggest IoU with the ground-truth bounding box for backpropagation.

RoI Pooling layer

The RoI Pooling layer is just a type of max-pooling, where the pool size is dependent on the input size. Doing this ensures that the output is always of the same size. This layer is used because the fully-connected layer always expects the same input size, but input regions to the FC layer may have different sizes.

The inputs of the RoI layer will be the proposals and the last convolution layer activations. For example, consider the following input image and its proposals:

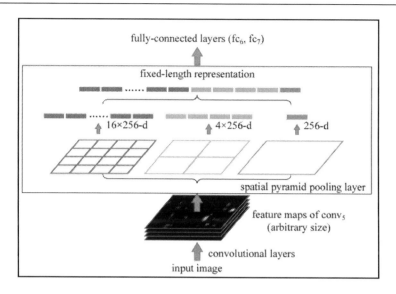

Here, we have a table summarizing the differences between methods:

	R-CNN	Fast R-CNN	Faster R-CNN
Test time per image	50 seconds	2 seconds	0.2 seconds
Speed-up	1x	25x	250x
Accuracy	66%	66.9%	66.9%

Conversion from traditional CNN to Fully Convnets

Something very important to efficient object detectors, that improves the reuse of computation, is to use sliding windows convolutionally. In order to this,we will convert all FC layers to CONV layers, as shown in the next figure.

The purpose of implementing our network this way is that they can use a bigger image as input than what they are originally designed for and at the same time share computations to make it all more efficient. The name of this type of network, where all the FC layers are converted to CONV layers, is called fully convolutional network (FCN).

The basic technique to convert an FC layer to a CONV layer is to use the kernel size as big as the input spatial dimensions and to use the number of filters to match the number of outputs on the FC layer. In this example we expect a 14x14x3 input image.

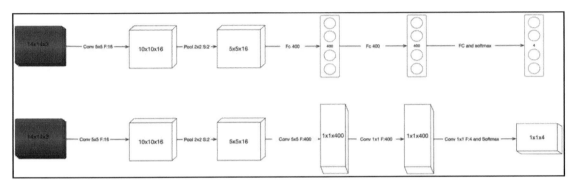

If we take the for example, training a fully convolutional network with input patches of 100 x 100 and test with input images sized 2,000 x 2,000, the effect would be to have a sliding window of size 100 x 100 running across the 2000 x 2000 image. When using using bigger input volumes (like in this example) the output of the FCN will be a volume where each cell corresponds to one slide of the 100x100 window patch on the original input image.

Now, every time we use an input image bigger than the original training input, the effect will be like we're actually sliding the classifier throughout the image but with less computation. Doing it this way, we make the sliding window convolutionally in one step through one forward pass of the CNN:

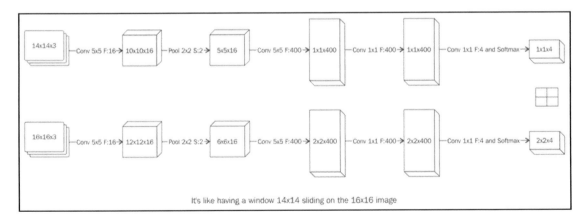

Single Shot Detectors – You Only Look Once

In this section we will move on to a slightly different kind of object detector called a single shot detectors. Single shot detectors try posing object detection as a regression problem. One of the main architectures under this category is the YOLO architecture (You Only Look Once) which we will explore in more detail now.

The main idea of the YOLO network is to optimise the computation of predictions at various locations in the input image without using any sliding windows. In order to achieve this, the network outputs feature map in form of a grid of size $N \times N$ cells.

Each cell has B*5+C entries. Where "B" is the number of bounding boxes per cell, C is the number of class probabilities and 5 is the elements for each bounding box (x, y :center point coordinates of bounding box with respect to the cell in which it is located , w-width of the bounding box with respect to original image, h-height of the bounding box with respect to original image, confidence score: how likely object is present in the bounding box).

We define Confidence score as:

$$P_c = P_r(object). IOU(Prediction_{box}, GroundTruth_{box})$$

If there is no object present in the cell then will zero. Otherwise will be equal to the IOU between the ground truth box and the predicted box.

Note that each cell of the grid is responsible for predicting a fixed number of bounding boxes.

Figure below depicts how the cell entries look like as an output from YOLO network which predicts a tensor of shape (N, N, B*5+C). The last conv layer of the network will output feature map of same size as the grid dimensions.

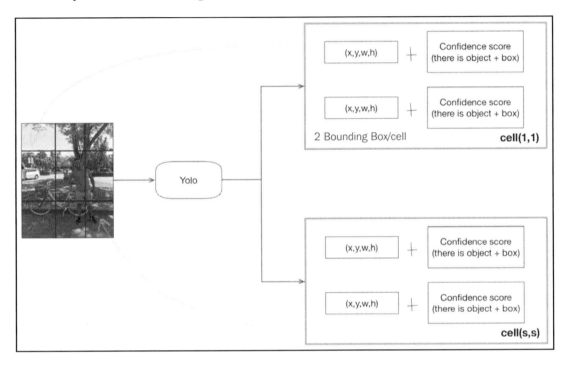

The center coordinates and the height and width of the bounding box are normalized between [0 , 1]. The following figure shows an example of how to calculate these coordinates:

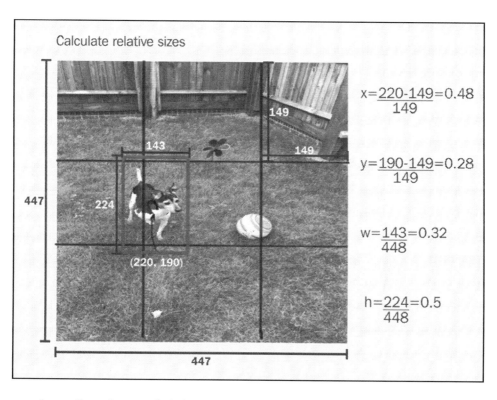

The network predicts class probabilities, bounding boxes, and confidence for these boxes for each of these cells.

The actual YOLO network has 24 convolutional layers, followed by 2 fully connected layers. However, Fast YOLO network is 9 layers, as shown:

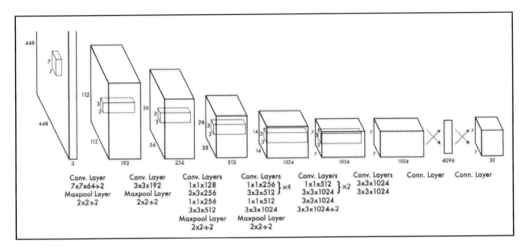

Another important point is that each object will be assigned to one grid cell alone (based on this center and the cell distance) even if it appears to be on multiple cells.

Currently, we can imagine that the number of objects that can be detected on the image will be the grid size; later, we will see how to handle multiple objects per grid cell. (Anchor boxes)

Creating training set for Yolo object detection

To create the training set for YOLO, a grid of the same size as output feature map prediction from the YOLO network is placed on each training input image. For each cell within the grid, we create a target vector Y of length B*5+C (that is, the same as output feature map grid cell size in the preceding section).

Let's take an example training image and see how we create target vector for cells in grid on the image:

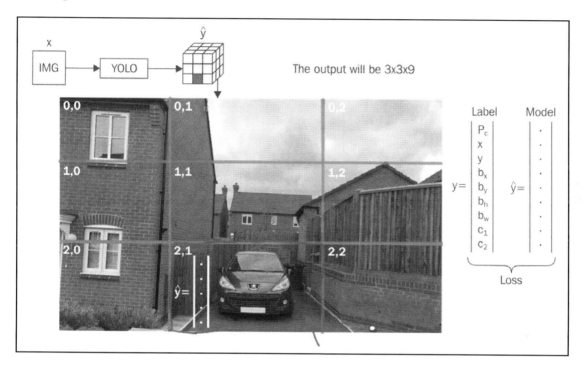

In the preceding illustration, consider that we choose the cell based on the shortest distance of the object center (in the image, the back car's center is closest to the green cell). If we look at the training image above we notice that object of class of interest is only present in one cell that is cell number 8. Rest of the cells 1-7 and 9 don't have any object of interest. The target vector for each cell will have 16 entries and look like following:

$$Y = \begin{bmatrix} p_c \\ x \\ y \\ h \\ w \\ c_1 \\ c_2 \\ c_3 \\ p_c \\ x \\ y \\ h \\ w \\ c_1 \\ c_2 \\ c_3 \end{bmatrix} \longrightarrow \begin{bmatrix} 0 \\ ? \\ ? \\ ? \\ ? \\ ? \\ ? \\ ? \\ 0 \\ ? \\ ? \\ ? \\ ? \\ ? \\ ? \\ ? \end{bmatrix} \begin{bmatrix} 0 \\ ? \\ ? \\ ? \\ ? \\ ? \\ ? \\ ? \\ 0 \\ ? \\ ? \\ ? \\ ? \\ ? \\ ? \\ ? \end{bmatrix} \begin{bmatrix} 0 \\ ? \\ ? \\ ? \\ ? \\ ? \\ ? \\ ? \\ 0 \\ ? \\ ? \\ ? \\ ? \\ ? \\ ? \\ ? \end{bmatrix} \begin{bmatrix} 0 \\ ? \\ ? \\ ? \\ ? \\ ? \\ ? \\ ? \\ 0 \\ ? \\ ? \\ ? \\ ? \\ ? \\ ? \\ ? \end{bmatrix} \begin{bmatrix} 0 \\ ? \\ ? \\ ? \\ ? \\ ? \\ ? \\ ? \\ 0 \\ ? \\ ? \\ ? \\ ? \\ ? \\ ? \\ ? \end{bmatrix} \begin{bmatrix} 0 \\ ? \\ ? \\ ? \\ ? \\ ? \\ ? \\ ? \\ 0 \\ ? \\ ? \\ ? \\ ? \\ ? \\ ? \\ ? \end{bmatrix} \begin{bmatrix} 0 \\ ? \\ ? \\ ? \\ ? \\ ? \\ ? \\ ? \\ 0 \\ ? \\ ? \\ ? \\ ? \\ ? \\ ? \\ ? \end{bmatrix} \begin{bmatrix} 1 \\ x \\ y \\ h \\ w \\ 1 \\ 0 \\ 0 \\ 0 \\ ? \\ ? \\ ? \\ ? \\ ? \\ ? \\ ? \end{bmatrix} \begin{bmatrix} 0 \\ ? \\ ? \\ ? \\ ? \\ ? \\ ? \\ ? \\ 0 \\ ? \\ ? \\ ? \\ ? \\ ? \\ ? \\ ? \end{bmatrix}$$

cell: 1   2   3   4   5   6   7   8   9

First entry which is confidence score for the presence of class P_c which is 0 for both anchor boxes in cells which don't have any object. Rest of the values will be *don't cares*. Cell number 8 has an object and the bounding box of object has high IOU.

The final volume of the target vector output from ConvNet after training for the input training image of size NxM will be 3x3x16 (On this toy example)

The label information for each image in your dataset will just include the objects' center coordinates and their bounding boxes. It's your responsibility while implementing the code to make it match the output vector of your network; these include tasks like the ones listed:

1. Transforming the image space into your grid space for each center point
2. Transform the bounding box dimensions on the image space to grid space dimensions
3. Find which cell is closest to your object on the image space

If we multiply each cell class's probability with the confidence for each bounding box, we will get some detections that can be filtered by another algorithm (Non-Maxima Suppression).

Let's define confidence as something that reflects the presence or absence of an object of any class on the cell. (Note that if there is no object on the cell, the confidence should be zero, and if there is an object, the confidence should be the IoU):

$$Confidence = Pr(object) * IoU(predicted_{rect}, groundtruth_{rect})$$

We also need to define a conditional class probability; given the presence of an object $P(class|Pr)$, we want this because we don't want the loss function to penalize a wrong class prediction if there is no object on the cell. The network only predicts one set of class probabilities per cell, regardless of the number of boxes, B.

Evaluating detection (Intersection Over Union)

Before we move further, we need to know how to measure whether our model detected an object correctly or not; for this, we calculate the Intersection Over Union (IoU) that will return a number, telling us how good our detection was based on some reference (Ground Truth). IoU is calculated by dividing the area where a detection and ground-truth box overlap with each over by the total area covered by the detection and ground-truth box:

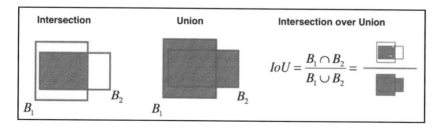

Here is an example of a poor, good, and excellent IoU:

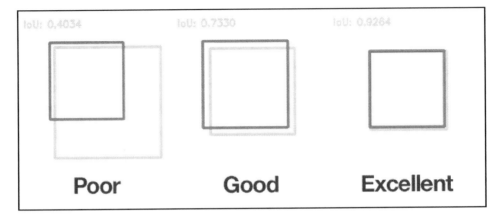

By convention, if the IoU is bigger than 0.5, we consider that both boxes match and in this case, a detection is a true positive.

An IoU of zero means that the boxes don't intersect, and an IoU of one means a perfect match.

On our detector, if a cell has more than one anchor boxes, IoU helps to choose which one is responsible for object .We choose the anchor which has highest IoU with the ground truth.

Here's the Python code for IoU:

```python
def iou_non_vectorized(box1, box2):
    # If one of the rects are empty return 0 (No intersect)
    if box1 == [] or box2 == []:
        return 0

    # size of intersect divided by size of union of 2 rects
    # Get rectangle areas format (left,top,right,bottom)
    box_1_area = (box1[2] - box1[0] + 1) * (box1[3] - box1[1] + 1)
    box_2_area = (box2[2] - box2[0] + 1) * (box2[3] - box2[1] + 1)

    # Get the intersection coordinates (x1,y1,x2,y2)
    intersect_x1 = max(box1[0], box2[0])
    intersect_y1 = max(box1[1], box2[1])
    intersect_x2 = min(box1[2], box2[2])
    intersect_y2 = min(box1[3], box2[3])

    # Calculate intersection area
    intersect_area = (intersect_x2 - intersect_x1 + 1) * (intersect_y2 -
intersect_y1
```

```
    + 1)

    return intersect_area / float(box_1_area + box_2_area - intersect_area)
```

We can also change this to a vectorized form on Tensorflow

```
def tf_iou_vectorized(self, box_vec_1, box_vec_2):
    def run(tb1, tb2):
        # Break the boxes rects vector in sub-vectors
        b1_x1, b1_y1, b1_x2, b1_y2 = tf.split(box_vec_1, 4, axis=1)
        b2_x1, b2_y1, b2_x2, b2_y2 = tf.split(box_vec_2, 4, axis=1)

        # Get rectangle areas format (left,top,right,bottom)
        box_vec_1_area = (b1_x2 - b1_x1 + 1) * (b1_y2 - b1_y1 + 1)
        box_vec_2_area = (b2_x2 - b2_x1 + 1) * (b2_y2 - b2_y1 + 1)

        xA = tf.maximum(b1_x1, tf.transpose(b2_x1))
        yA = tf.maximum(b1_y1, tf.transpose(b2_y1))
        xB = tf.minimum(b1_x2, tf.transpose(b2_x2))
        yB = tf.minimum(b1_y2, tf.transpose(b2_y2))

        interArea = tf.maximum((xB - xA + 1), 0) * tf.maximum((yB - yA + 1),
0)

        iou = interArea / (box_vec_1_area + tf.transpose(box_vec_2_area) -
interArea)

        return iou

    op = run(self.tf_bboxes1, self. tf_bboxes2)
    self.sess.run(op, feed_dict={self.tf_bboxes1: box_vec_1,
self.tf_bboxes2: box_vec_2})
    tic = time()
    self.sess.run(op, feed_dict={self.tf_bboxes1: box_vec_1,
self.tf_bboxes2: box_vec_2})
    toc = time()
    return toc - tic
```

We can also change this to a vectorized form on TensorFlow, as shown:

```
def tf_iou_vectorized(self, box_vec_1, box_vec_2):
    def run(tb1, tb2):
        # Break the boxes rects vector in sub-vectors
        b1_x1, b1_y1, b1_x2, b1_y2 = tf.split(box_vec_1, 4, axis=1)
        b2_x1, b2_y1, b2_x2, b2_y2 = tf.split(box_vec_2, 4, axis=1)
    # Get rectangle areas format (left,top,right,bottom)
        box_vec_1_area = (b1_x2 - b1_x1 + 1) * (b1_y2 - b1_y1 + 1)
        box_vec_2_area = (b2_x2 - b2_x1 + 1) * (b2_y2 - b2_y1 + 1)
        xA = tf.maximum(b1_x1, tf.transpose(b2_x1))
```

```
        yA = tf.maximum(b1_y1, tf.transpose(b2_y1))
        xB = tf.minimum(b1_x2, tf.transpose(b2_x2))
        yB = tf.minimum(b1_y2, tf.transpose(b2_y2))
        interArea = tf.maximum((xB - xA + 1), 0) * tf.maximum((yB - yA + 1),
0)
        iou = interArea / (box_vec_1_area + tf.transpose(box_vec_2_area) -
interArea)
        return iou
    op = run(self.tf_bboxes1, self. tf_bboxes2)
    self.sess.run(op, feed_dict={self.tf_bboxes1: box_vec_1, self.tf_bboxes2:
box_vec_2})
    tic = time()
    self.sess.run(op, feed_dict={self.tf_bboxes1: box_vec_1, self.tf_bboxes2:
box_vec_2})
    toc = time()
    return toc - tic
```

Filtering output

More often than not, your model in practice will return multiple detection windows for the same object. To handle this, we use an algorithm called Non-Maximum Suppression. This algorithm filters these multiple boxes using the "IoU and presence of object" as heuristics. Here's how it works:

1. Discard all boxes with a low probability of containing an object (pc < 0.6)
2. Select the box with the biggest probability of having an object (pc on our label)
3. Discard all boxes with a high overlap with the selected box (IoU > 0.5)
4. Repeat steps 2 and 3 until all detections are either discarded or selected

We will use the Non-Maximum suppression on the prediction time on our detector:

Tensorflow already has a function that implements the non-maxima suppression algorithm, called `tf.image.non_max_suppression`.

Anchor Box

Anchor boxes predefined template boxes of certain height and width ratio. These are used in YOLO to help detect multiple objects from a single grid cell. We define the shape of boxes based on rough geometry of type of objects that can be detected.

Currently, as explained, our model will be able to detect only one object per grid cell, but in most cases, you may have multiple objects per cell. Remember that we consider the cell closest to the object to be the center:

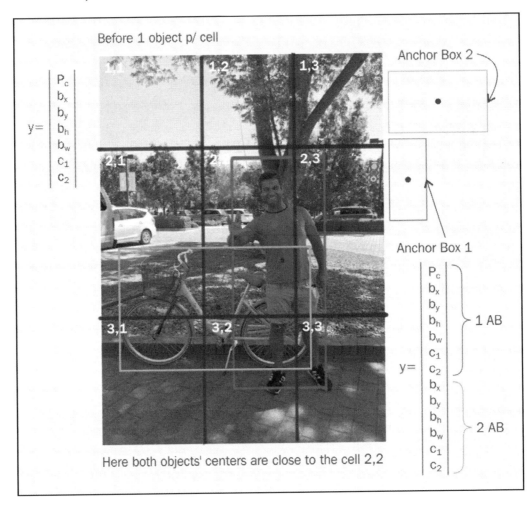

To solve this, we need Anchor points; basically, we will add to our output depth volume a predefined bounding box; then, during training, we choose the objects with the center closest to a particular cell and choose the bounding box with the biggest IoU to the anchor box. In practice, the idea of anchor boxes make the network generalize the detection better, due to the fact that several subnetworks will be responsible for looking for other objects on the same cell.

Testing/Predicting in Yolo

Consider the image in previous car image as our test image now. The output of prediction vector for each cell would be:

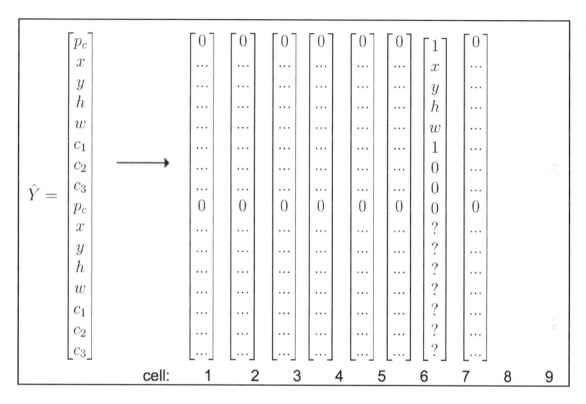

Note that **...** entries mean that there will be some random values in predicted vector even for cells which don't have any object. However in cell 8 the predicted values for x, y, h, w will be hopefully nearly accurate.

At final stage we can filter multiple predicted bounding boxes in each cell using Non-maxima suppression algorithm.

Detector Loss function (YOLO loss)

As the localizer, the YOLO loss function is broken into three parts: the one responsible for finding the bounding-box coordinates, the bounding-box score prediction, and the class-score prediction. All of them are Mean-Squared error losses and are modulated by some scalar meta-parameter or IoU score between the prediction and ground truth:

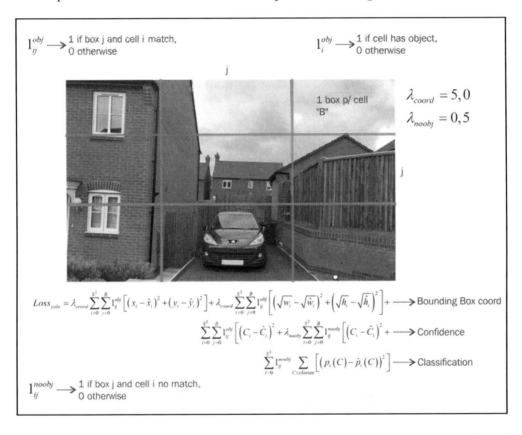

The member *1ij* obj member is used to modulate the loss based on the presence of an object on a particular cell i, j:

- If an object is present in grid cell i and the jth bounding box having the highest IoU: 1
- Otherwise: 0

Also, *1ij noobj* is just the opposite.

Loss Part 1

$$\lambda_{coord} \sum_{i=0}^{S^2} \sum_{j=0}^{B} 1_{ij}^{obj} [(x_i - \hat{x}_i)^2 + (y_i - \hat{y}_i)^2]$$

The first part computes the loss related to the predicted bounding box position coordinates (x, y). $(\hat{x}, \hat{y})$ are the bounding box coordinates for ground truth data in training set.

$\lambda_{coord} = 5.0$ represents a constant used to give more penalty when there is a mistake. B is the number of bounding boxes. And S^2 is the number of cells in the grid.

Similar equation is used to handle the bounding box width/height

$$\lambda_{coord} \sum_{i=0}^{S^2} \sum_{j=0}^{B} 1_{ij}^{obj} [(\sqrt{w_i} - \sqrt{\hat{w}_i})^2 + (\sqrt{h_i} - \sqrt{\hat{h}_i})^2]$$

Square root on the width and height in loss function equation is used to reflect that small deviations in small boxes matter more than large boxes. In general term this part of loss penalizes the bounding boxes with inaccurate height and width.

Loss Part 2

This part of the loss function computes loss related to the confidence score for each bounding box predictor.

$$\sum_{i=0}^{S^2} \sum_{j=0}^{B} 1_{ij}^{obj} [(C_i - \hat{C}_i)^2 + \lambda_{noobj} \sum_{i=0}^{S^2} \sum_{j=0}^{B} 1_{ij}^{noobj} [(C_i - \hat{C}_i)^2$$

C is the confidence score (term modulated by the presence of an object) $\hat{C}$ is the IOU of the predicted bounding box with ground truth box. The parameter $\lambda_{noobj} = 0.5$ is used to make the loss care less about the confidence when there is no object.

Loss Part 3

The classification loss is the last part of loss function.

$$\sum_{i=0}^{S^2} 1_i^{obj} \sum_{C \in classes} [(p_i(C) - \hat{p}_i(C))^2]$$

This loss is the sum of squared error loss for classification. Again the term 1_i^{obj} is 1 when there is a object on a cell, and 0 otherwise. The idea is that we don't take into account the classification error when there is on object.

The 1_i^{obj} , $1_{i,j}^{obj}$, $1_{i,j}^{noobj}$, terms serve to mask the loss on the case that we have an object on the ground-truth and have an object on the model output for a particular cell. Also the same is truth when the ground-truth and the model output doesn't match.

So for example when for a particular cell we don't have a match our loss will be:

$$L_{\text{NOMATCH}} = 0.5. \sum_{i=0}^{S^2} \sum_{j=0}^{B} [(C_i - \hat{C}_i)^2$$

And when we have a match:

$$L_{\text{MATCH}} = 5. \sum_{i=0}^{S^2} \sum_{j=0}^{B} [(x_i - \hat{x}_i)^2 + (y_i - \hat{y}_i)^2] + 5. \sum_{i=0}^{S^2} \sum_{j=0}^{B} [(\sqrt{w_i} - \sqrt{\hat{w}_i})^2 + (\sqrt{h_i} - \sqrt{\hat{h}_i})^2] +$$

$$\sum_{i=0}^{S^2} \sum_{j=0}^{B} [(C_i - \hat{C}_i)^2 +$$

$$\sum_{i=0}^{S^2} \sum_{C \in \text{classes}} [(p_i(C) - \hat{p}_i(C))^2]$$

During implementation in practice you will try to vectorize this loss and avoid for-loops and improve performance, this is specially true for libraries like Tensorflow.

Here's the TensorFlow implementation of YOLO loss:

```
def loss_layer(self, predicts, labels, scope='loss_layer'):
    with tf.variable_scope(scope):
        predict_classes = tf.reshape(predicts[:, :self.boundary1],
[self.batch_size, self.cell_size, self.cell_size, self.num_class])
        predict_scales = tf.reshape(predicts[:,
self.boundary1:self.boundary2], [self.batch_size, self.cell_size,
self.cell_size, self.boxes_per_cell])
        predict_boxes = tf.reshape(predicts[:, self.boundary2:],
[self.batch_size, self.cell_size, self.cell_size, self.boxes_per_cell, 4])

        response = tf.reshape(labels[:, :, :, 0], [self.batch_size,
self.cell_size, self.cell_size, 1])
        boxes = tf.reshape(labels[:, :, :, 1:5], [self.batch_size,
self.cell_size, self.cell_size, 1, 4])
```

```
        boxes = tf.tile(boxes, [1, 1, 1, self.boxes_per_cell, 1]) /
self.image_size
        classes = labels[:, :, :, 5:]

        offset = tf.constant(self.offset, dtype=tf.float32)
        offset = tf.reshape(offset, [1, self.cell_size, self.cell_size,
self.boxes_per_cell])
        offset = tf.tile(offset, [self.batch_size, 1, 1, 1])
        predict_boxes_tran = tf.stack([(predict_boxes[:, :, :, :, 0] +
offset) / self.cell_size,
                                       (predict_boxes[:, :, :, :, 1] +
tf.transpose(offset,
(0, 2, 1, 3))) / self.cell_size,
                                       tf.square(predict_boxes[:, :, :, :,
2]),
                                       tf.square(predict_boxes[:, :, :, :,
3])])
        predict_boxes_tran = tf.transpose(predict_boxes_tran, [1, 2, 3, 4,
0])

        iou_predict_truth = self.tf_iou_vectorized(predict_boxes_tran,
boxes)

        # calculate I tensor [BATCH_SIZE, CELL_SIZE, CELL_SIZE,
BOXES_PER_CELL]
        object_mask = tf.reduce_max(iou_predict_truth, 3, keep_dims=True)
        object_mask = tf.cast((iou_predict_truth >= object_mask),
tf.float32) * response

        # calculate no_I tensor [CELL_SIZE, CELL_SIZE, BOXES_PER_CELL]
        noobject_mask = tf.ones_like(object_mask, dtype=tf.float32) -
object_mask

        boxes_tran = tf.stack([boxes[:, :, :, :, 0] * self.cell_size -
offset,
                               boxes[:, :, :, :, 1] * self.cell_size -
tf.transpose(offset, (0, 2, 1, 3)),
                                       tf.sqrt(boxes[:, :, :, :, 2]),
                                       tf.sqrt(boxes[:, :, :, :, 3])])
        boxes_tran = tf.transpose(boxes_tran, [1, 2, 3, 4, 0])

        # class_loss
        class_delta = response * (predict_classes - classes)
        class_loss = tf.reduce_mean(tf.reduce_sum(tf.square(class_delta),
axis=[1, 2, 3]), name='class_loss') * self.class_scale

        # object_loss
        object_delta = object_mask * (predict_scales - iou_predict_truth)
```

```
        object_loss = tf.reduce_mean(tf.reduce_sum(tf.square(object_delta),
axis=[1, 2, 3]), name='object_loss') * self.object_scale

        # noobject_loss
        noobject_delta = noobject_mask * predict_scales
        noobject_loss =
tf.reduce_mean(tf.reduce_sum(tf.square(noobject_delta), axis=[1, 2, 3]),
name='noobject_loss') * self.noobject_scale

        # coord_loss
        coord_mask = tf.expand_dims(object_mask, 4)
        boxes_delta = coord_mask * (predict_boxes - boxes_tran)
        coord_loss = tf.reduce_mean(tf.reduce_sum(tf.square(boxes_delta),
axis=[1, 2, 3, 4]), name='coord_loss') * self.coord_scale
```

Semantic segmentation

In semantic segmentation, the goal is to label each individual pixel of an image according to what object class that pixel belongs to. The final result is a bitmap where each pixel will belong to a certain class:

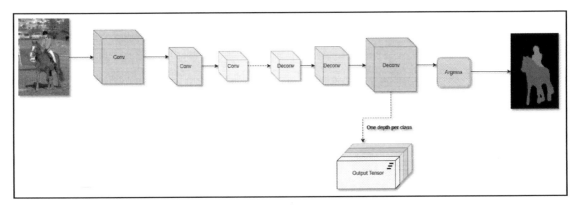

There are several popular CNN architectures that have been shown to do well at the segmentation task. Most of them are variants of a class of model called an autoencoder, which we will look at in detail in Chapter 6, *Autoencoders, Variational Autoencoders, and Generative Models*. For now, their basic idea is to first spatially reduce the input volume to some compressed representation and then recover the original spatial size:

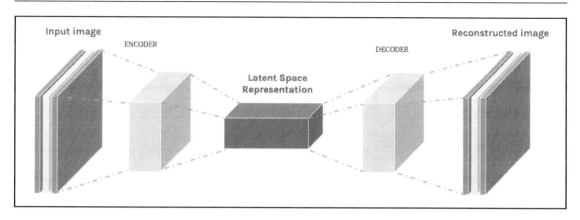

In order to increase the spatial size, there are some common operations that are used, which include the following:

- Max Unpooling
- Deconvolution/Transposed Convolution
- Dilated/Atrous Convolution

There's also a new variant of softmax that is used in the semantic segmentation task that we will learn about, which is called **spatial softmax**.

In this section, we will learn about two popular models that perform well at semantic segmentation and have very straightforward architectures to understand; they are as listed:

- FCN (Fully Convolutional Networks)
- Segnet

Some other implementation details that need to be addressed are these:

- The final upsampling layer (Deconv) needs to have as many filters as classes to segment, and your label "colors" need to match the indexes inside this last layer, otherwise you may have some NaN issues during training
- We need an Argmax layer to select the pixel with the strongest probability on the output tensor (during prediction time only)
- Our loss needs to take into account all the pixels on the output tensor

Max Unpooling

The unpooling operation is used to revert the effect of the max pooling operation; the idea is just to work as an upsampler. This operation has been used on some older papers and is not used so much anymore due to the fact that you also need a CONV layer to inpaint (low pass filter) the results of the upsampling:

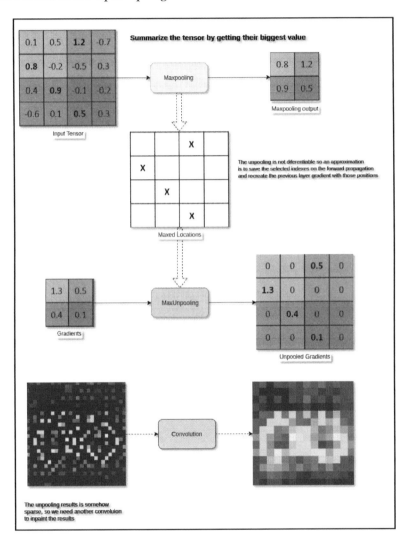

Deconvolution layer (Transposed convolution)

This operation is rather badly named as deconvolution, which implies that it is the inverse operation to convolution, but that is not actually the case. The more apt name is transposed convolution or fractionally-strided convolution.

This layer type offers you a learnable way of upsampling an input volume and can be used every time that you need to intelligently project an input feature map to a higher spatial space. Some use cases include the following:

- Upsampling (strided transposed convolution) == UNPOOL+CONV
- Visualizing salient maps
- As part of autoencoders

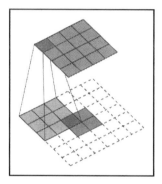

In Tensorflow, we have access to transposed convolution within `tf.layers`. The following example will take an input of spatial size 14 x 14 and put it through the `conv2d_transpose` layer, where the output spatial size becomes 28 x 28:

```
# input_im has spatial dimensions 14x14 in this example
output = tf.layers.conv2d_transpose(inputs=input_im, filters=1,
kernel_size=4, strides=2, padding='same')
```

Care has to be taken when selecting `kernel_size`, strides, and padding scheme, as these will all affect the output spatial size.

The loss function

As mentioned, the loss function for segmentation models will basically be an extension of the classification loss, but working spatially throughout the whole output vector:

$$Loss_{seg} = \frac{1}{Batch} \sum_{b=1}^{batch} \sum_{p=1}^{pixel} \sum_{c=1}^{class} label_{p,k} ln(Softmax(output_{tensor}))$$

```
# Segmentation problems often uses this "spatial" softmax (Basically we
want to classify each pixel)
with tf.name_scope("SPATIAL_SOFTMAX"):
    loss = tf.reduce_mean((tf.nn.sparse_softmax_cross_entropy_with_logits(
        logits=model_out,labels=tf.squeeze(labels_in,
squeeze_dims=[3]),name="spatial_softmax")))
```

The below image depicts the implementation of Fully Convolutional Networks for Semantic Segmentation:

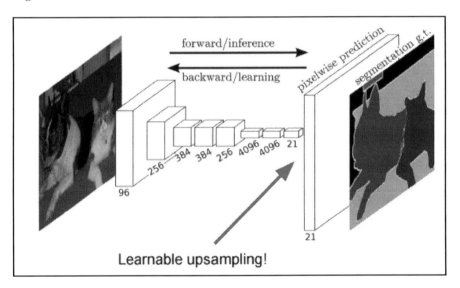

The below image shows the SegNet architecture:

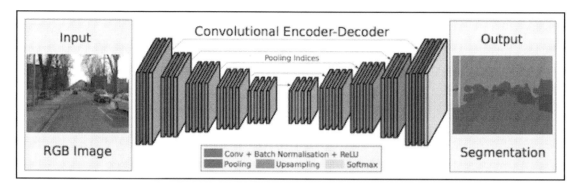

Labels

As mentioned earlier, the labels in the segmentation problem are one-dimensional images with a value at each pixel that matches the index of the output volume depth:

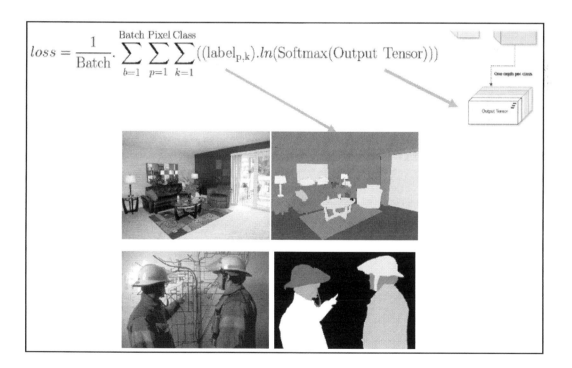

Improving results

One technique that is normally used to improve the results of the segmentation output is to use Conditional Random Fields (CRF) at the post-processing stage, by taking into account pure RGB features of the image and probabilities produced by our network:

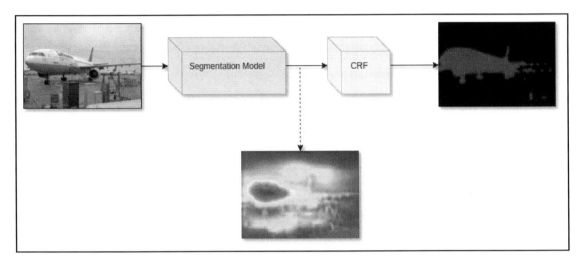

Instance segmentation

Instance segmentation is the last thing we will look at in this chapter. In many ways, it can be thought of as a fusion of object detection and semantic segmentation. However, it is definitely a step up in difficulty compared to those two problems.

With instance segmentation, the idea is to find every occurrence, what is called an instance, of a desired object or objects within an image. Once these are found, we want to segment off each instance from the other, even if they belong to the same class of objects. In other words, labels are both class-aware (such as car, sign, or person) and instance-aware (such as car 1, car 2, or car 3).

The result of instance segmentation will look something like this:

The similarity between this and semantic segmentation is clear; we still label pixels according to what object they belong to. However, while semantic segmentation has no knowledge of how many times a certain object occurs within an image instance, segmentation does.

This ability to know how many instances of an object are in an image also makes this problem similar to object detection. However, object detection produces a much coarser object boundary, which means occluded objects are more likely to be missed, which shouldn't happen with instance segmentation.

Mask R-CNN

One recent network architecture that went some way in making this problem easier to solve by providing a simple, flexible model architecture is Mask R-CNN. Published in 2017, the architecture looks at extending the capabilities of faster R-CNN:

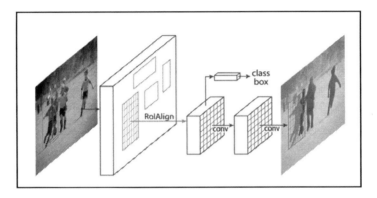

It takes the existing faster R-CNN model and tries to solve the instance-segmentation problem by adding a branch to the model that is responsible for predicting object masks in parallel to the classification and bounding-box regression head. This architecture proved effective and achieved top honors in all the COCO challenges at the time of publishing.

Summary

In this chapter, we learned the basics of object localization, detection and segmentation. We also discussed the most famous algorithms related to those topics.

In the next chapter, we will discuss some common network architectures.

5
VGG, Inception Modules, Residuals, and MobileNets

So far, we have discussed all the necessary building blocks for us to be able to implement solutions to common problems such as image classification and detection. In this chapter, we will talk about the implementation of some common model architectures that have shown high performance in many of these common tasks. These architectures have remained popular since they were first created, and they continue to be widely used today.

By the end of this chapter, you will gain an understanding of the different types of CNN models that exist, along with their use cases in a variety of different computer vision problems. While implementing these models, you will learn how these models were designed and the advantages for each of them. Finally, we will talk about how we can modify these architectures in order to make training and performance/efficiency better.

In summary, this chapter will cover the following topics:

- How to improve parameter efficiency
- How to implement the VGG nets in TensorFlow
- How to implement Inception nets in TensorFlow
- How to implement Residual nets in TensorFlow
- How to implement an architecture that is friendlier for mobile devices

Substituting big convolutions

Before we jump in, we will first learn about the techniques that can reduce the number of parameters a model uses. This is important, firstly because it should improve your network's ability to generalize, as it will need less training data fed into it to utilize the number of parameters present in the model. Secondly, having less parameters means more hardware efficiency, as less memory will be needed.

Here, we will start by explaining one important technique for reducing model parameters, cascading several small convolutions together. In the diagram that follows, we have two 3x3 convolution layers. If we look at the second layer, on the right of the diagram, working back, we can see that one neuron in the second layer has a 3x3 receptive field:

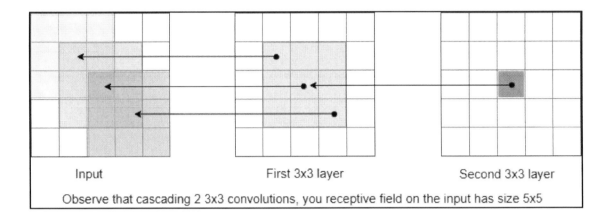

Observe that cascading 2 3x3 convolutions, you receptive field on the input has size 5x5

When we say "receptive field," we mean the area that it can see from a previous layer. In this example, a 3x3 area is needed to create one output, hence a 3x3 receptive field.

Working back another layer, each element of that 3x3 area also has a 3x3 receptive field on the input. So, if we combine the receptive field for all those nine elements together, then we can see that total receptive field created on the input is of size 5x5.

So, in simpler words, cascading smaller convolutions together can get the same receptive field as using a bigger one. That means we can replace big convolutions with a cascade of small ones.

Note that this substitution cannot be done on the very first convolution layer acting on the input image due to the depth mismatch between the first convolution layer and the input file depth (depths of outputs need to be consistent): Also observe on the image how we calculate the number of parameters per layer.

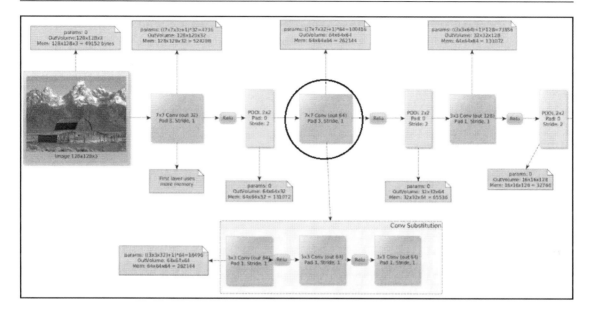

In the preceding diagram, we substitute one 7x7 convolution by three 3x3 convolutions. Let's calculate for ourselves to see that less parameters are used.

Imagine a 7x7 size convolution, with C filters, being used on an input volume of shape WxHxC. We can calculate the number of weights in the filters as follows:

$$num_{weights_{7x7}} = C * 7 * 7 * C = 49C^2$$

Now, instead, if we cascade three 3x3 convolutions (substituting the 7x7 convolution), we could calculate its number of weights as follows:

$$num_{weights_{3x3}} = 3 * (C * 3 * 3 * C) = 27C^2$$

Here, we can see that there are less parameters than earlier!

Also observe that between each of those three convolution layers, we place ReLu activations. Doing this introduces more non-linearities into the model than we would have had using just a single large convolution layer. This added depth (and non-linearities) is a good thing, as it means the network can compose more concepts together and increase its capacity for learning!

The trend in most new successful models is to replace all large filters with many smaller convolutions (usually size 3x3) cascaded together. As explained before, we get two huge benefits from doing this. Not only does it reduce the number of parameters, it also increases the depth and number of non-linearities in your network, which is a good thing for increasing its learning capacity.

Substituting the 3x3 convolution

It's also possible to simplify the 3x3 convolution with a mechanism called a bottleneck. Similar to earlier, this will have the same representation of a normal 3x3 convolution, but with less parameters and more non-linearities.

The bottleneck works by replacing a 3x3 convolution layer with C filters with the following:

- A 1x1 convolution with C/2 filters
- A 3x3 convolution with C/2 filters
- A 1x1 convolution with C filters

An example in action is given here:

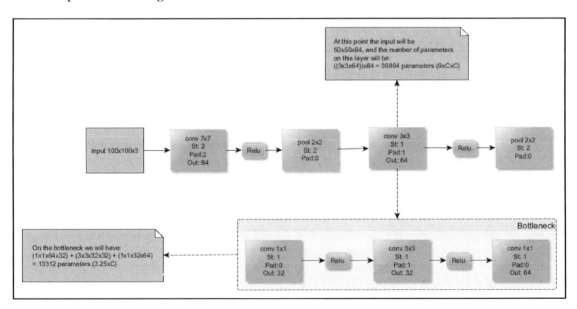

From this example, we will calculate the number of parameters to show the reduction this bottleneck has. We get the following:

$$num\,m_{weight} = ((1 * 1 * C)\frac{C}{2}) + ((3 * 3 * \frac{C}{2})\frac{C}{2}) + ((1 * 1 * \frac{C}{2})C) = 3.25 * C^2$$

This is less than the parameters we would get if we just used a 3x3 convolution layer:

$$num\,m_{weight} = ((3 * 3 * C)C) = 9 * C^2$$

Some network architectures, such as residual networks (which we will see later), use the bottleneck technique to again reduce the number of parameters and add more non-linearities.

VGGNet

Created by the **Visual Geometry Group** (**VGG**) at Oxford University, VGGNet was one of the first architectures to really introduce the idea of stacking a much larger number of layers together. While AlexNet was considered deep when it first came out with its seven layers, this is now a small amount compared to both VGG and other modern architectures.

VGGNet uses only very small filters with a spatial size of 3x3, compared to AlexNet, which had up to 11x11. These 3x3 convolution filters are frequently interspersed with 2x2 max pooling layers.

Using such small filters means that the neighborhood of pixels seen is also very small. Initially, this might give the impression that local information is all that is being taken into account by the model. Interestingly though, by stacking small filters one after another, it gives the same "receptive field" as a single large filter. For example, stacking three lots of 3x3 filters will have the same receptive field as one 7x7 filter.

This insight of stacking filters brings the bonus of being able to have a deeper structure (which we will see is usually always better) that retains the same receptive field size, while also reducing the number of parameters. This idea is further explored later in the chapter.

Architecture

Next, we see the architecture of the VGGNet, specifically the VGG-16 flavor that contains, unsurprisingly, 16 layers. All convolution layers have filters of spatial size 3x3, and the number of filters in the convolution layers increases from 64 to 512 as we go deeper into the network.

The simple modular design of stacking two or three convolutional layers followed by pooling allows the network to be easily increased or reduced in size. As a result, the VGG successfully created and tested versions with 11, 13, and 19 layers:

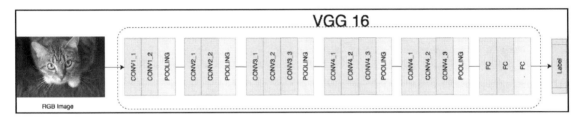

Parameters and memory calculation

One of the coolest features of VGG is that due to its small kernel size in the conv layers, the amount of parameters used is low. If we remember from `Chapter 2`, *Deep Learning and Convolutional Neural Networks*, the amount of parameters in a convolution layer (minus the bias) can be calculated as follows:

$$n_{params} = ((F.F.depth_{input}) + 1).num_{filters}$$

So, for example, the first layer would have the following parameters:

$$n_{params} = ((3.3.3) + 1).64 = 1792$$

Beware, though, that this low number of parameters is not the case when it comes to the fully connected (dense) layers at the end of the model, which is usually the place where we can find a lot of the model parameters. This is especially true if, like in VGGNet, you stack multiple dense layers one after the other.

For example, the first dense layer would have this amount of parameters:

$$n_{params} = (input_{tensor_{shape}} * num_{outputs})$$

$$n_{params} = (7 * 7 * 512 * 4096) = 102,760,448$$

That's more than six times all the parameters up to that point!

As mentioned earlier, you need to have a large number of samples in your training dataset to consume your model parameters, so it's better to avoid this explosion of parameters with excessive use of fully connected layers. Luckily, people found out that VGGNet works pretty much the same if we have just one dense layer at the end rather than three. So, removing these fully connected layers removes a huge number of parameters from the model, while not reducing performance much. As a result, this is what we recommend that you do as well if you decide to implement a VGGNet.

Code

Next, we present the function responsible for building the VGG-16 model graph in Tensorflow. VGGNet, like all the models in this chapter, was designed to classify the 1,000 classes of the Imagenet challenge, which is why this model outputs a vector of size 1,000. Obviously, this can be easily changed for your own datasets, as follows:

```
def build_graph(self):

    self.__x_ = tf.placeholder("float", shape=[None, 224, 224, 3], name='X')

    self.__y_ = tf.placeholder("float", shape=[None, 1000], name='Y')


    with tf.name_scope("model") as scope:
        conv1_1 = tf.layers.conv2d(inputs=self.__x_, filters=64,
kernel_size=[3, 3],

                                    padding="same", activation=tf.nn.relu)

        conv2_1 = tf.layers.conv2d(inputs=conv1_1, filters=64,
kernel_size=[3, 3],

                                    padding="same", activation=tf.nn.relu)


        pool1 = tf.layers.max_pooling2d(inputs=conv2_1, pool_size=[2, 2],
strides=2)


        conv2_1 = tf.layers.conv2d(inputs=pool1, filters=128,
kernel_size=[3, 3],
```

```
                                    padding="same", activation=tf.nn.relu)

        conv2_2 = tf.layers.conv2d(inputs=conv2_1, filters=128,
kernel_size=[3, 3],

                                        padding="same", activation=tf.nn.relu)

        pool2 = tf.layers.max_pooling2d(inputs=conv2_2, pool_size=[2, 2],
strides=2)

        conv3_1 = tf.layers.conv2d(inputs=pool2, filters=256, kernel_size=[3,
3],

                                        padding="same", activation=tf.nn.relu)

        conv3_2 = tf.layers.conv2d(inputs=conv3_1, filters=256,
kernel_size=[3, 3],

                                        padding="same", activation=tf.nn.relu)

        conv3_3 = tf.layers.conv2d(inputs=conv3_2, filters=256,
kernel_size=[3, 3],

                                        padding="same", activation=tf.nn.relu)



        pool3 = tf.layers.max_pooling2d(inputs=conv3_3, pool_size=[2, 2],
strides=2)



        conv4_1 = tf.layers.conv2d(inputs=pool3, filters=512,
kernel_size=[3, 3],

                                        padding="same", activation=tf.nn.relu)

        conv4_2 = tf.layers.conv2d(inputs=conv4_1, filters=512,
kernel_size=[3, 3],

                                        padding="same", activation=tf.nn.relu)

        conv4_3 = tf.layers.conv2d(inputs=conv4_2, filters=512,
kernel_size=[3, 3],

                                        padding="same", activation=tf.nn.relu)
```

```
        pool4 = tf.layers.max_pooling2d(inputs=conv4_3, pool_size=[2, 2],
strides=2)



        conv5_1 = tf.layers.conv2d(inputs=pool4, filters=512,
kernel_size=[3, 3],

                                   padding="same", activation=tf.nn.relu)
        conv5_2 = tf.layers.conv2d(inputs=conv5_1, filters=512,
kernel_size=[3, 3],

                                   padding="same", activation=tf.nn.relu)
        conv5_3 = tf.layers.conv2d(inputs=conv5_2, filters=512,
kernel_size=[3, 3],

                                   padding="same", activation=tf.nn.relu)



        pool5 = tf.layers.max_pooling2d(inputs=conv5_3, pool_size=[2, 2],
strides=2)



        pool5_flat = tf.reshape(pool5, [-1, 7 * 7 * 512])

        # FC Layers (can be removed)

        fc6 = tf.layers.dense(inputs=pool5_flat, units=4096,
activation=tf.nn.relu)

        fc7 = tf.layers.dense(inputs=fc6, units=4096, activation=tf.nn.relu)

        # Imagenet has 1000 classes

        fc8 = tf.layers.dense(inputs=fc7, units=1000)

        self.predictions = tf.nn.softmax(self.fc8, name='predictions')
```

More about VGG

In 2014, VGG achieved the second place in the Imagenet Classification challenge and the first place in the Imagenet Localization challenge. As we saw, the VGGNet design choice of stacking many small convolution layers allows for a deeper structure that performs better while having less parameters (if we remove the unnecessary fully connected layers). This design choice is so effective in creating power and efficient networks that pretty much all modern architectures copy this idea and will rarely, if at all, use large filters.

The VGG model is proven to work well in a lot of tasks, and because of its simple architecture, it's a go-to model to start experimenting with or adapting to the needs of your problem. However, it does have the following issues to be aware of:

- By using only 3x3 layers, especially on the first layer, the amount of compute is not suitable to mobile solutions
- Even deeper VGG structures don't work as well due to vanishing gradient problems, as mentioned in the previous chapters
- The huge amount of FC layers in the original design is overkill in terms of parameters, which not only slows the model down but also makes it easier to have overfitting problems
- The use of many pooling layers, which is currently not considered good design

GoogLeNet

While VGGNet came second in the 2014 Imagenet Classification challenge, the next model we will talk about, GoogLeNet, was the winner that year. Created by Google, it introduced an important way to make networks deeper and reduce the number of parameters at the same time. They called what they came up with the `Inception` module. This module populates the majority of the GoogLeNet model.

GoogLeNet has 22 layers and almost 12 times fewer parameters than AlexNet. Thus, in addition to being far more accurate, it is also much quicker than AlexNet. The motivation for the `Inception` module creation was to make a deeper CNN so that highly accurate results could be achieved and for the model to be usable in a smartphone. For this, the calculation budget needed to be roughly 1.5 billion multiply-adds in the prediction phase:

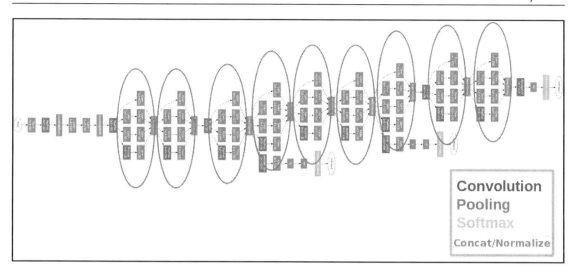

Inception module

The Inception module (or block of layers) aims to cover a large area but also keep a fine resolution in order to see the important local information in images as well. In addition to creating deeper networks, the inception block introduces the idea of parallel convolutions. What we meant by this is that in-parallel convolutions of different sizes are performed on the output of the previous layer.

A naive view of the inception layer can be seen here:

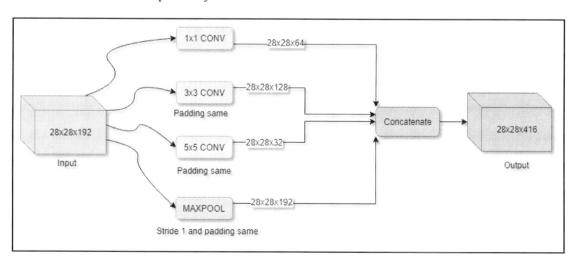

Basically, the idea of the inception block is to use all available kernel sizes and operations to cover the most information possible and let the backpropagation decide what to use based on your data. The only problem seen in the preceding diagram is the computation cost, so the graph will be a bit different in practice.

Consider the 5x5 branch we saw previously, and let's check its computing cost:

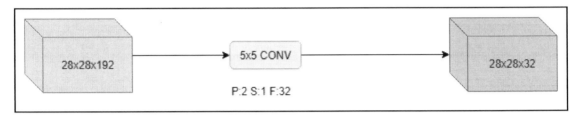

$$\#MAC = 5 * 5(\frac{28 + 2 * 2 - 5}{1} + 1) * (\frac{28 + 2 * 2 - 5}{1} + 1) * 192 * 32 * 1 = 120422400$$

Now, consider the following change; we add a 1x1 CONV to transform the 5x5 CONV input depth from 192 to 16:

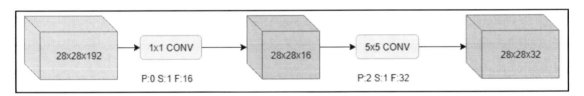

$$\#MAC_{5x5} = 5 * 5(\frac{28 + 2 * 2 - 5}{1} + 1) * (\frac{28 + 2 * 2 - 5}{1} + 1) * 16 * 32 * 1 = 10035200$$

$$\#MAC_{1x1} = 1 * 1(\frac{28 - 1}{1} + 1) * (\frac{28 - 1}{1} + 1) * 192 * 16 * 1 = 2408448$$

$$\#MAC = \#MAC_{1x1} + \#MAC_{5x5} = 12443648$$

If you observe, the compute is now 10 times more efficient. The 1x1 layer squeezes the massive depth (bottleneck) before sending to the 5x5 CONV layer.

Considering this bottleneck change, the true inception layer is a little more complex:

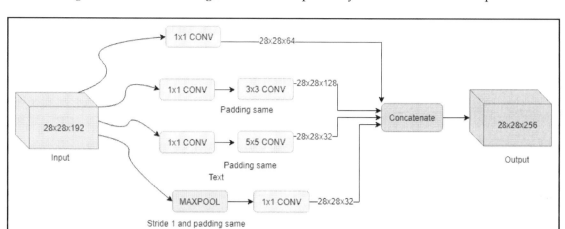

Also, in some implementations, you may notice people trying to use Batchnorm or dropout inside the inception block.

Googlenet will be just many inception blocks in cascade; in this piece of code, we show how to create an inception block:

```
# Reference: https://github.com/khanrc/mnist/blob/master/inception.py

import tensorflow as tf




def inception_block_a(x, name='inception_a'):

    # num of channels: 384 = 96*4

    with tf.variable_scope(name):

        # Pooling part

        b1 = tf.layers.average_pooling2d(x, [3,3], 1, padding='SAME')

        b1 = tf.layers.conv2d(inputs=b1, filters=96, kernel_size=[1, 1],
padding="same", activation=tf.nn.relu)
```

```
        # 1x1 part

        b2 = tf.layers.conv2d(inputs=x, filters=96, kernel_size=[1, 1],
padding="same", activation=tf.nn.relu)


        # 3x3 part

        b3 = tf.layers.conv2d(inputs=x, filters=64, kernel_size=[1, 1],
padding="same", activation=tf.nn.relu)

        b3 = tf.layers.conv2d(inputs=b3, filters=96, kernel_size=[3, 3],
padding="same", activation=tf.nn.relu)


        # 5x5 part

        b4 = tf.layers.conv2d(inputs=x, filters=64, kernel_size=[1, 1],
padding="same", activation=tf.nn.relu)

        # 2 3x3 in cascade with same depth is the same as 5x5 but with less
parameters

        # b4 = tf.layers.conv2d(inputs=b4, filters=96, kernel_size=[5, 5],
padding="same", activation=tf.nn.relu)

        b4 = tf.layers.conv2d(inputs=b4, filters=96, kernel_size=[3, 3],
padding="same", activation=tf.nn.relu)

        b4 = tf.layers.conv2d(inputs=b4, filters=96, kernel_size=[3, 3],
padding="same", activation=tf.nn.relu)


        concat = tf.concat([b1, b2, b3, b4], axis=-1)

        return concat
```

More about GoogLeNet

The main advantage of GoogLeNet is that it is more accurate than VGG, while using much fewer parameters and less compute power. The main disadvantage is still the gradient vanishing that would occur if we begin stacking lots and lots of inception layers, and also the rather complicated design of the whole network with multiple branches and losses.

Residual Networks

In previous sections it was shown that the depth of a network is a crucial factor that contributes in accuracy improvement (see VGG). It was also shown in Chapter 3, *Image Classification in TensorFlow*, that the problem of vanishing or exploding gradients in deep networks can be alleviated by correct weight initialization and batch normalization. Does this mean however, that the more layers we add the more accurate the system we get is? The authors in *Deep Residual Learning for Image Recognition* form Microsoft research Asia have found that accuracy gets saturated as soon as the network gets 30 layers deep. To solve this problem they introduced a new block of layers called the residual block, which adds the output of the previous layer to the output of the next layer (refer to the figure below). The Residual Net or ResNet has shown excellent results with very deep networks (greater than even 100 layers!), for example the 152-layer ResNet which won the 2015 LRVC image recognition challenge with top-5 test error of 3.57. Deeper networks such as ResNets have also proven to work better than wider ones such as those including Inception modules (e.g. GoogLeNet).

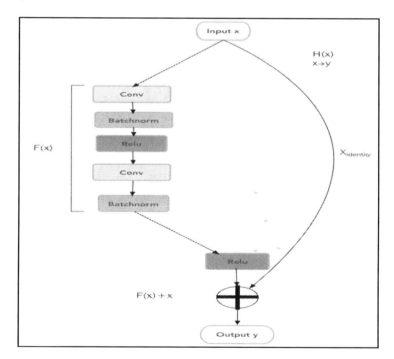

Let us see in more detail how a residual block looks and the intuition behind its functionality. If we have an input x and an output y then there is a non linear function $H(x)$ that maps x to y. Suppose that the function $H(x)$ can be approximated by two stacked nonlinear convolution layers. Then the residual function $F(X) = H(x) - x$ can be approximated as well. We can equivalently write that $H(x) = F(x) + x$, $F(x)$ where represents two stacked non linear layers and x the identity function (input=output).

More formally, for a forward pass through the network, if x is a tensor from $l-2$ layer and W_{l-1} and W_l are the weight matrices of the current and previous layers, then the input y to the next layer $l+1$ is

$$y = g(F(x) + x) = g(W_l g(W_{l-1} x) + x)$$

Where $g(\bullet)$ is a nonlinear activation function such as ReLu and $F(x) = W_l g(W_{l-1} x)$, i.e. a two layer stacked convolution . The ReLu function can be added before or after the addition of x. The residual block should consist of 2 or more layers as a one-layer block has no apparent benefit.

To understand the intuition behind this concept let us assume that we have a shallow trained CNN and its deeper counterpart that has identical layers to that of the shallow CNN, and some more layers randomly inserted in between. In order to have a deep model that has at least similar performance to the shallow one, the additional layers must approximate identity functions. However learning an identity function with a stack of CONV layers is harder than pushing the residual function to zero. In other words if the identity function is the optimal solution, it is easy to achieve $F(x) = 0$ and consequently $H(x) = x$.

Another way to think of this is that during training, a particular layer will learn a concept not only from the previous layer but also from the other layers before it. This should work better than learning a concept only from the previous layer.

Implementation wise, we should be careful to make sure that x and $F(x)$ are the same size.

The alternative way to view the importance of the residual block is that we're going to have a "highway" (addition block) for the gradients that will avoid the vanishing gradient problem as the gradients get added!

The following code will show you how to create the residual block, which is the main building block of residual networks:

```
# Reference
#
https://github.com/tensorflow/tensorflow/blob/master/tensorflow/examples/le
arn/resnet.py
import tensorflow as tf
from collections import namedtuple

# Configurations for each bottleneck group.
BottleneckGroup = namedtuple('BottleneckGroup',
                             ['num_blocks', 'num_filters',
'bottleneck_size'])
groups = [
    BottleneckGroup(3, 128, 32), BottleneckGroup(3, 256, 64),
    BottleneckGroup(3, 512, 128), BottleneckGroup(3, 1024, 256)
]

# Create the bottleneck groups, each of which contains `num_blocks`
# bottleneck groups.
for group_i, group in enumerate(groups):
    for block_i in range(group.num_blocks):
        name = 'group_%d/block_%d' % (group_i, block_i)

        # 1x1 convolution responsible for reducing dimension
        with tf.variable_scope(name + '/conv_in'):
            conv = tf.layers.conv2d(
                net,
                filters=group.num_filters,
                kernel_size=1,
                padding='valid',
                activation=tf.nn.relu)
            conv = tf.layers.batch_normalization(conv, training=training)

        with tf.variable_scope(name + '/conv_bottleneck'):
            conv = tf.layers.conv2d(
                conv,
                filters=group.bottleneck_size,
                kernel_size=3,
                padding='same',
                activation=tf.nn.relu)
            conv = tf.layers.batch_normalization(conv, training=training)

        # 1x1 convolution responsible for restoring dimension
        with tf.variable_scope(name + '/conv_out'):
            input_dim = net.get_shape()[-1].value
            conv = tf.layers.conv2d(
```

```
        conv,
        filters=input_dim,
        kernel_size=1,
        padding='valid',
        activation=tf.nn.relu)
    conv = tf.layers.batch_normalization(conv, training=training)

    # shortcut connections that turn the network into its counterpart
    # residual function (identity shortcut)
    net = conv + net
```

MobileNets

We will finish this chapter with a new family of CNN that not only has good accuracy, but is lighter and works faster on mobile devices.

Created by Google, MobileNet's key feature is that it uses a different "sandwich" form of convolution block. Instead of the usual (CONV, BATCH_NORM, RELU), it splits 3x3 convolutions up into a 3x3 depthwise convolution, followed by a 1x1 Pointwise CONV. They call this block a depthwise separable convolution.

This factorization reduces the computation and the model size:

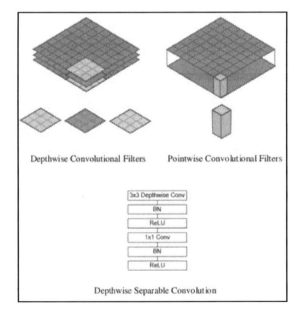

Depthwise Convolutional Filters   Pointwise Convolutional Filters

3x3 Depthwise Conv
BN
ReLU
1x1 Conv
BN
ReLU

Depthwise Separable Convolution

Depthwise separable convolution

This new convolution block (`tf.layers.separable_conv2d`) consists of two main parts: a depthwise convolution layer, followed by a 1x1 pointwise convolution layer. This block differs from the normal convolution in a couple of ways:

- In the normal convolution layer, each filter F will be applied to all channels on the input channel at the same time (F is applied to each channel and then summed)
- This new convolution F is applied on each channel separately, and the results get concatenated to some intermediate tensor (how much is controlled by the Depth Multiplier, DM parameter)

The depthwise convolution is extremely efficient relative to standard convolution. However, it only filters input channels, and it does not combine them to create new features.

Now, the depthwise output tensor will be mapped to some desired output channel depth using a 1x1 conv layer that will do the mixing between channels that normally occurs in the standard convolution layers. The difference is that the DM parameter can be used to throw away some information. Again, the 1x1 conv has been used just to adapt volume sizes.

Control parameters

MobileNets uses two hyperparameters to help control the trade-off between accuracy and speed, allowing for a network that is suitable for any device you want to target. The two hyperparameters are as follows:

- **Width Multiplier**: Controls the Depthwise CONVs accuracy by uniformly reducing the number filters used throughout the network
- **Resolution Multiplier**: Simply scales down the input image to different sizes

More about MobileNets

MobileNets has some of the best accuracy, speed, and parameter ratios for any neural network design.

However, currently there is no good (fast) implementation of depthwise convolutions for running on a GPU; as a result, training will likely be slower than using a normal convolution operation. However, where this network really shines at the moment is in small CPU designs, where the increased efficiency is more visible.

Summary

In this chapter, we introduced you to different convolutional neural network designs that have proven their effectiveness and, as a result, are widely used. We started by introducing the VGGNet model by VGG at Oxford University. Next, we moved on to GoogLeNet by Google, before finally talking about Microsoft's Residual Net. In addition, we showed you a more advanced and new type of convolution that is featured in a model design called MobileNet. Throughout, we talked about the different properties and design choices that make each of these networks so good, such as skip connections, stacking small filters, or inception modules. Finally, code was given showing you how to write out these networks in TensorFlow.

In the next chapter, we will talk about a new kind of model, called a generative model, which will allow us to generate data.

6
Autoencoders, Variational Autoencoders, and Generative Adversarial Networks

This chapter will cover a slightly different kind of model to what we have seen so far. All the models presented until now belong to a type of model called a discriminative model. Discriminative models aim to find the boundaries between different classes. They are interested in finding $P(Y|X)$—the probability of output Y given some input X. This is the natural probability distribution to work with for classification, as you usually want to find a label Y, given some input X.

However, there is another type of model called a generative model. Generative models are built to model the distributions of different classes. They are interested in finding $P(Y, X)$—the probability distribution of output Y and input X occurring together. In theory, if you can capture the probability distribution of classes in your data, you will know more about it, and you will be able to calculate $P(Y|X)$ using Bayes rule.

Generative models belong to the category of unsupervised learning algorithms. Unsupervised means that we don't need to have labeled data.

In this chapter, some key topics we will learn about are as listed:

- Autoencoders
- Variational autoencoders
- Generative adversarial networks
- Implementing various generative models for generating handwritten digits

Why generative models

In the following illustration, we can see the main difference between generative models and discriminative models. With discriminative models, we generally try to find ways of separating or "discriminating" between different classes in our data. However, with generative models, we try to find out the probability distribution of our data. In the illustration, the distributions are represented by the large blue and yellow blobs that contain smaller circles. If we learn this distribution from our data, we will be able to sample or "generate" new data points that should belong to it like the red triangle.

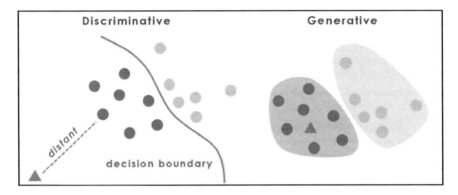

Trying to capture the probability distribution of a dataset has the following use cases:

- Pretrain a model with unlabeled data
- Augment your dataset (in theory, if you capture the probability distribution of your data, you can generate more data)
- Compress your data (lossy)
- Create some sort of simulator (for example, a quadcopter can be controlled with four inputs; if you capture this data and train a generative model on it, you can learn the dynamics of the drone)

The expectation when using generative models is that if we're able to create new data similar to the original input data, our model must have learned something about the distribution of our data.

Generative neural network models are trained to produce data samples that resemble the training set. As the number of model parameters is smaller than the dimensionality of the training data, the models are forced to discover efficient data representations .

Autoencoders

The first generative model we will look at is the autoencoder model. An autoencoder is a simple neural network that is composed of two parts: an **encoder** and a **decoder**. The idea is that the encoder part will compress your input into a smaller dimension. From this smaller dimension, it then tries to reconstruct the input using the decoder part of the model. This smaller dimension is often called by many names such as latent space, hidden space, an embedding, or a coding.

If the autoencoder is able to reproduce its input, then, in theory, this latent space should encode all the important information needed to represent the original data, but with the advantage of being a smaller dimension than the input. The encoder can be thought of as a way of compressing the input data while the decoder is the way to uncompress it. We can see what a simple autoencoder looks like in the following illustration. Our latent space or coding is the part in the middle labeled z.

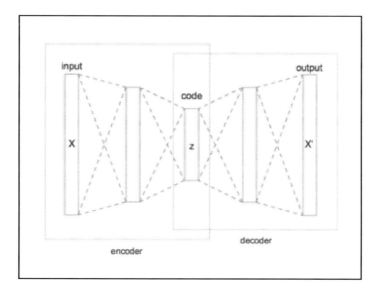

Traditionally, in an autoencoder, the layers that make up the network are just fully connected layers, but autoencoders can be extended to images as well by using convolutional layers. Just as earlier, the encoder will compress the input image to a smaller representation, and the decoder will try its best to recover the information. The difference is that the encoder is now a CNN that compresses the data into a feature vector, rather than an ANN with fully connected layers, and the decoder will use transposed convolution layers to recreate the image from the encoding.

An example of an autoencoder working on images is given here. For the decoder part of

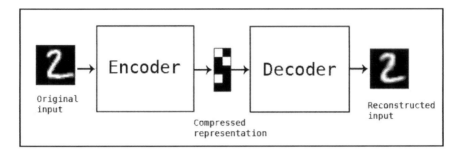

With any autoencoder, the loss function will guide both the encoder and decoder to reconstruct the input. A common loss to use is the L2 loss between the output of the autoencoder and the input of the network. One question that we should ask ourselves now is, "Is it a good idea to use L2 loss to compare images?". If you take the following images, even though they look quite different, they do in fact all have the same *L2* distance from each other:

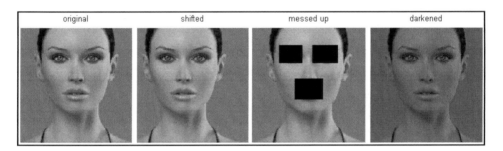

This shows that things like L2 loss can't always be relied upon when you are using it to compare images, so you should keep this in mind when working with it.

Convolutional autoencoder example

The following TensorFlow code will build a convolutional autoencoder model for the MNIST dataset. This first part of the code will construct the graph of your model, the encoder and the decoder. In the code, we highlight the part of the model whose output will be our latent vector:

```
class CAE_CNN(object):
    def __init__(self, img_size = 28, latent_size=20):
        self.__x = tf.placeholder(tf.float32, shape=[None, img_size *
img_size], name='IMAGE_IN')
```

```
        self.__x_image = tf.reshape(self.__x, [-1, img_size, img_size, 1])


    with tf.name_scope('ENCODER'):
        ##### ENCODER
        # CONV1: Input 28x28x1 after CONV 5x5 P:2 S:2 H_out: 1 +
(28+4-5)/2 = 14, W_out= 1 + (28+4-5)/2 = 14
        self.__conv1_act = tf.layers.conv2d(inputs=self.__x_image,
strides=(2, 2),
                                                    filters=16, kernel_size=[5,
5], padding="same", activation=tf.nn.relu)

        # CONV2: Input 14x14x16 after CONV 5x5 P:0 S:2 H_out: 1 +
(14+4-5)/2 = 7, W_out= 1 + (14+4-5)/2 = 7
        self.__conv2_act = tf.layers.conv2d(inputs=self.__conv1_act,
strides=(2, 2),
                                                    filters=32, kernel_size=[5,
5], padding="same", activation=tf.nn.relu)

    with tf.name_scope('LATENT'):
        # Reshape: Input 7x7x32 after [7x7x32]
        self.__enc_out = tf.reshape(self.__conv2_act,
[tf.shape(self.__x)[0], 7 * 7 * 32])
        self.__guessed_z = tf.layers.dense(inputs=self.__enc_out,
                                        units=latent_size,
activation=None, name="latent_var")
        tf.summary.histogram("latent", self.__guessed_z)


    with tf.name_scope('DECODER'):
        ##### DECODER (At this point we have 1x18x64
        self.__z_develop = tf.layers.dense(inputs=self.__guessed_z,
                                        units=7 * 7 * 32,
activation=None, name="z_matrix")
        self.__z_develop_act = tf.nn.relu(tf.reshape(self.__z_develop,
[tf.shape(self.__x)[0], 7, 7, 32]))

        # DECONV1
        self.__conv_t2_out_act =
tf.layers.conv2d_transpose(inputs=self.__z_develop_act,
                                                        strides=(2,
2), kernel_size=[5, 5], filters=16,
padding="same", activation=tf.nn.relu)

        # DECONV2
        # Model output
        self.__y =
tf.layers.conv2d_transpose(inputs=self.__conv_t2_out_act,
                                                        strides=(2,
```

```
2), kernel_size=[5, 5], filters=1,
padding="same", activation=tf.nn.sigmoid)

            # We want the output flat for using on the loss
            self.__y_flat = tf.reshape(self.__y, [tf.shape(self.__x)[0], 28
* 28])
```

The code snippet related to the convolutional autoencoder loss is as follows:

```
with tf.name_scope("CAE_LOSS"):
    # L2 loss
    loss = tf.losses.mean_squared_error(labels=model_in,
predictions=model_out_flat)

# Solver configuration
with tf.name_scope("Solver"):
    train_step = tf.train.AdamOptimizer(0.0001).minimize(loss)
```

Uses and limitations of autoencoders

Autoencoders are cool in their simplicity, but they are somewhat limited in what they can do. One potential use of theirs is to pretrain a model (given that you have your model as the encoder part and that you are able to create an anti-model as the decoder). The use of autoencoders can be good for pretraining, as you can take your dataset and train your autoencoder to reconstruct it. Once trained, you can use the weights of the encoder and then fine-tune them to your intended task.

Another use is as a form of compression for your data if it isn't too complicated. You can use the autoencoder to reduce the dimensionality down to two or three dimensions and then try to visualize your inputs in the latent space to see whether it shows you anything useful.

One limitation of autoencoders, however, is that they cannot be used to generate more data for us. This is because we don't know how to create new latent vectors to feed to the decoder; the only way is to use the encoder on input data. We will now look at modification to the autoencoder that looks to help solve this issue.

Variational autoencoders

Our first true generative model, which can create more data that resembles the training data, will be the **variational autoencoder** (**VAE**). The VAE looks like the normal autoencoder but with a new constraint that will force our compressed representation (latent space) to follow a zero mean and unit variance Gaussian distribution.

The idea behind forcing this constraint on the latent space is that when we want to use our VAE to generate new data, we can just create sample vectors that come from a unit Gaussian distribution and give them to the trained decoder. It is this constraint on the latent space vector that is the difference between VAE and normal autoencoders. This constraint allows us a way to create new latent vectors than can be fed to the decoder to generate data.

The following figure shows that the VAE looks exactly the same in structure as the autoencoder, except for the constraint on the hidden space:

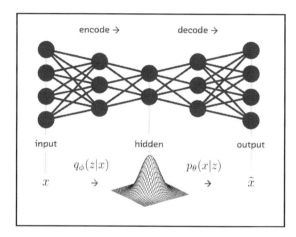

Parameters to define a normal distribution

We need two parameters to keep track and to enforce our VAE model to produce a normal distribution in the latent space:

- **Mean** (should be zero)
- **Standard deviation** (should be one)

In the following diagram, we have example of normal distributions with different mean and standard deviation values. With just these two values, we can produce a normal distribution that we can sample from:

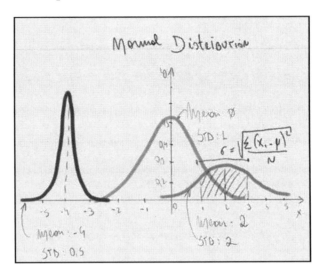

VAE loss function

In the VAE, our loss function is composed of two parts:

- **Generative loss**: This loss compares the model output with the model input. This can be the losses we used in the autoencoders, such as L2 loss.
- **Latent loss**: This loss compares the latent vector with a zero mean, unit variance Gaussian distribution. The loss we use here will be the KL divergence loss. This loss term penalizes the VAE if it starts to produce latent vectors that are not from the desired distribution.

The following screenshot shows the loss for the VAE and that it is a combination of the generative loss and a loss on the latent space:

```
generation_loss = mean(square(generated_image - real_image))
latent_loss = KL-Divergence(latent_variable, unit_gaussian)
loss = generation_loss + latent_loss
```

Kullback-Leibler divergence

The KL divergence loss is one that will produce a number indicating how close two distributions are to each other.

The closer two distributions get to each other, the lower the loss becomes. In the following graph, the blue distribution is trying to model the green distribution. As the blue distribution comes closer and closer to the green one, the KL divergence loss will get closer to zero.

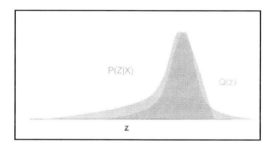

Training the VAE

In order for us to train the VAE and use the KL divergence loss, we will first need to play around with how we generate the latent vectors. Rather than having the encoder produce a latent vector exactly directly, we will make the encoder produce two vectors. The first will be a vector μ of mean values, and the second will be a vector σ of standard deviation values. From these, we can create a third vector, where the *i*th element is sampled from a Gaussian distribution using the *i*th values of our μ and σ vectors as the mean and standard deviation for that Gaussian distribution. This third sampled vector is then sent to the decoder.

Our model now looks something like this:

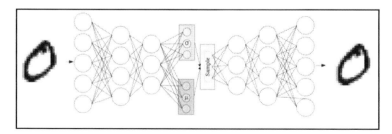

The mean and standard deviation blocks in the preceding diagram will be just normal fully connected layers that will learn how to return values we want by being guided by the KL loss function. The reason for changing how we get our latent vectors is because it allows us to calculate the KL divergence loss easily. The KL loss will now be the following, where `latent_mean` is **μ** and `latent_stddev` is **σ**:

```
0.5 * tf.reduce_sum(tf.square(latent_mean) + tf.square(latent_stddev) -
tf.log(tf.square(latent_stddev)) - 1, 1)
```

Unfortunately, there is this **Sample** block, which you can consider as a random generator node, that is not differentiable. This means we can't use backpropagation to train our VAE. What we need is something called the Reparameterization trick that will take out the sampling from the backpropagation flow.

The reparameterization trick

The idea of the reparameterization trick is to take out the random sample node from the backpropagation loop. It achieves this by taking a sample epsilon from a Gaussian distribution and then multiplying this by the result of our standard deviation vector **σ** and then adding **μ**. The formula for our latent vector is now this:

$$z^{(i,l)} = \mu^{(i)} + \sigma^{(i)} \odot \varepsilon_i$$

$$\varepsilon_i \sim N(0,1)$$

The produced latent vectors will be the same as before, but making this change now allows the gradients to flow back through to the encoder part of the VAE. The following diagram shows the VAE model before doing reparameterization on the left and after doing it on the right. The blue boxes are the two parts of our loss function. Looking at the diagram, you can see that our gradients can now flow backward, as we no longer have the red box (sample node) blocking the way:

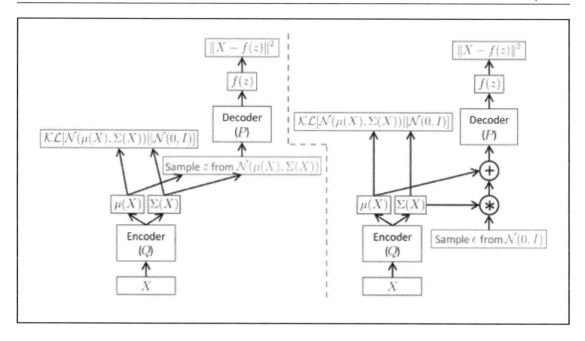

This is what this reparameterization looks like in TensorFlow:

```
# Add linear ops to produce mean and standard devation vectors
fc_mean = tf.layers.dense(self.__enc_out, units=latent_size,
activation=None, name="w_mean")
fc_stddev = tf.layers.dense(self.__enc_out, units=latent_size,
activation=None, name="w_stddev")

# Generate normal distribution with dimensions [Batch, latent_size]
sample_block = tf.random_normal([tf.shape(X)[0], latent_size], 0, 1,
dtype=tf.float32)
latent_z = fc_mean + (fc_stddev * sample_block)
```

Convolutional Variational Autoencoder code

We can now piece together everything and present TensorFlow code that will build a convolutional VAE for the MNIST dataset. We create a class for our VAE model and place the model in the __init__ method. The first part is the encoder of our model made up of two conv layers:

```
class VAE_CNN(object):
    def __init__(self, img_size=28, latent_size=20):
        self.__x = tf.placeholder(tf.float32, shape=[None, img_size *
```

```
img_size], name='IMAGE_IN')
        self.__x_image = tf.reshape(self.__x, [-1, img_size, img_size, 1])

    with tf.name_scope('ENCODER'):
        ##### ENCODER
        # CONV1: Input 28x28x1 after CONV 5x5 P:2 S:2 H_out: 1 +
(28+4-5)/2 = 14, W_out= 1 + (28+4-5)/2 = 14
        self.__conv1_act = tf.layers.conv2d(inputs=self.__x_image,
strides=(2, 2),
                                            filters=16, kernel_size=[5,
5], padding="same", activation=tf.nn.relu)

        # CONV2: Input 14x14x16 after CONV 5x5 P:0 S:2 H_out: 1 +
(14+4-5)/2 = 7, W_out= 1 + (14+4-5)/2 = 7
        self.__conv2_act = tf.layers.conv2d(inputs=self.__conv1_act,
strides=(2, 2),
                                            filters=32, kernel_size=[5,
5], padding="same", activation=tf.nn.relu)
```

This is followed by the part of the VAE responsible for creating the latent vector using our new reparameterization trick from earlier. We add logging of the final latent vector to check whether it produces vectors following unit Gaussian distribution as we expect:

```
    with tf.name_scope('LATENT'):
        # Reshape: Input 7x7x32 after [7x7x32]
        self.__enc_out = tf.reshape(self.__conv2_act,
[tf.shape(self.__x)[0], 7 * 7 * 32])

        # Add linear ops for mean and variance
        self.__w_mean = tf.layers.dense(inputs=self.__enc_out,
                                        units=latent_size,
activation=None, name="w_mean")
        self.__w_stddev = tf.layers.dense(inputs=self.__enc_out,
                                          units=latent_size,
activation=None, name="w_stddev")

        # Generate normal distribution with dimensions [B, latent_size]
        self.__samples = tf.random_normal([tf.shape(self.__x)[0],
latent_size], 0, 1, dtype=tf.float32)

        self.__guessed_z = self.__w_mean + (self.__w_stddev *
self.__samples)
    tf.summary.histogram("latent_sample", self.__guessed_z)
```

After this, we add the decoder part of our network, which consists of a fully connected layer, followed by two transposed convolution layers:

```
            with tf.name_scope('DECODER'):
                ##### DECODER
                # Linear layer
                self.__z_develop = tf.layers.dense(inputs=self.__guessed_z,
                                                    units=7 * 7 * 32,
    activation=None, name="z_matrix")
                self.__z_develop_act = tf.nn.relu(tf.reshape(self.__z_develop,
    [tf.shape(self.__x)[0], 7, 7, 32]))

                # DECONV1
                self.__conv_t2_out_act =
    tf.layers.conv2d_transpose(inputs=self.__z_develop_act,
                                                                strides=(2,
    2), kernel_size=[5, 5], filters=16,
    padding="same", activation=tf.nn.relu)

                # DECONV2
                # Model output
                self.__y =
    tf.layers.conv2d_transpose(inputs=self.__conv_t2_out_act,
                                                        strides=(2, 2),
    kernel_size=[5, 5], filters=1,
                                                        padding="same",
    activation=tf.nn.sigmoid)

                # Model output
                self.__y_flat = tf.reshape(self.__y, [tf.shape(self.__x)[0], 28
    * 28])
```

Separate from our model, we need to write out our final loss function that will be used to train the VAE. We can then pass this loss to our optimizer of choice to create our training step:

```
# Loss function

with tf.name_scope("VAE_LOSS"):
    # L2 loss (generative loss)
    generation_loss = tf.losses.mean_squared_error(labels=model_in,
predictions= model_out_flat)
    # KL Loss (latent loss)
    latent_loss = 0.5 * tf.reduce_sum(tf.square(z_mean) +
tf.square(z_stddev) - tf.log(tf.square(z_stddev)) - 1, 1)
    # Merge the losses
```

```
        loss = tf.reduce_mean(generation_loss + latent_loss)

# Solver
with tf.name_scope("Solver"):
    train_step = tf.train.AdamOptimizer(0.0001).minimize(loss)
```

Generating new data

After the VAE model is trained, we can chop off its decoder part and use this as a generator to generate new data for us. It will work by feeding it new latent vectors that come from a unit Gaussian distribution.

We present in TensorFlow the code responsible for build this generating VAE graph as follows:

```
class VAE_CNN_GEN(object):
    def __init__(self, img_size=28, latent_size=20):
        self.__x = tf.placeholder(tf.float32, shape=[None, latent_size],
name='LATENT_IN')
        with tf.name_scope('DECODER'):
            # Linear layer
            self.__z_develop = tf.layers.dense(inputs=self.__x,
                                               units=7 * 7 * 32,
activation=None, name="z_matrix")
            self.__z_develop_act = tf.nn.relu(tf.reshape(self.__z_develop,
[tf.shape(self.__x)[0], 7, 7, 32]))

            # DECONV1
            self.__conv_t2_out_act =
tf.layers.conv2d_transpose(inputs=self.__z_develop_act,
                                                             strides=(2,
2), kernel_size=[5, 5], filters=16,
padding="same", activation=tf.nn.relu)

            # DECONV2
            # Model output
            self.__y =
tf.layers.conv2d_transpose(inputs=self.__conv_t2_out_act,
                                                      strides=(2, 2),
kernel_size=[5, 5], filters=1,
                                                      padding="same",
activation=tf.nn.sigmoid)

    @property
    def output(self):
        return self.__y
```

```
@property
def input(self):
    return self.__x
```

Generative adversarial networks

Generative adversarial networks (**GAN**) are another very recent type of generative model that got attention due to their impressive results. A GAN is composed of two networks together: a generator network and a discriminator network. During training, they both play a zero-sum game, where the discriminator network tries to discover whether the images input to it are real or fake. At the same time, the generator network tries to create fake images that are good enough to fool the discriminator.

The idea is that after some time of training, both the discriminator and the generator become very good at their tasks. As a result, the generator is forced to try and create images that look closer and closer to the original dataset. To be able to do this, it must capture the probability distribution of the dataset.

The following diagram gives an overview of how this GAN model looks:

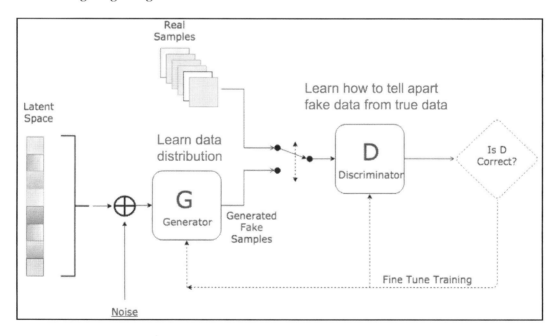

Both discriminator and generator will have their own loss function, but both of their losses depends on each other.

Let's summarize the two main blocks, or networks, of the GAN model:

- **Generator**: Create images similar to the *real images* dataset using a size N, 1-D vector as input (Choice of N is up to us)
- **Discriminator**: Verify that the image given to it is real or a fake generated one

Some practical usages for GANs are as follows:

- Use the discriminator network weights as the initialization for a different task similar to what we can do with autoencoders
- Use the generator network to create new images, possibly to augment your dataset, like we can do with the trained decoder of the VAE
- Use the discriminator as a loss function (potentially, better than L1/L2 for images) and can also be used back in the VAE
- Semi-supervised learning by mixing generated data with labeled data

We will now show you how to implement a very simple GAN in TensorFlow. Once it is trained, the generator part of our GAN can be used create MNIST handwritten digits from a 100 long vector of random noise. Let's get started!

The discriminator

The first thing we need is to create our discriminator network. For this, we stack several fully connected layers together. The discriminator takes as input a batch of 784 length vectors, which is our 28x28 MNIST images flattened. The output will be just a single number for each image, which is the score of how confident the discriminator is with regard to that image being a real image. We use Leaky ReLu as the activation function to prevent ReLu units from dying out.

We return raw logits, as the loss function will apply the sigmoid activation function for us to ensure that our discriminator output is between 0 and 1:

```
def discriminator(x):
    with tf.variable_scope("discriminator"):
        fc1 = tf.layers.dense(inputs=x, units=256,
activation=tf.nn.leaky_relu)
        fc2 = tf.layers.dense(inputs=fc1, units=256,
activation=tf.nn.leaky_relu)
        logits = tf.layers.dense(inputs=fc2, units=1)
        return logits
```

The generator

Now we create our generator network. The job of the generator is to take a vector of random noise as input and from this, produce an output image. For this example, we again use fully connected layers that will, at the end, produce an output of a 784 long vector that we can reshape to get our 28x28 image:

```
def generator(z):
    with tf.variable_scope("generator"):
        fc1 = tf.layers.dense(inputs=z, units=1024, activation=tf.nn.relu)
        fc2 = tf.layers.dense(inputs=fc1, units=1024,
activation=tf.nn.relu)
        img = tf.layers.dense(inputs=fc2, units=784,
activation=tf.nn.tanh)
        return img
```

We use the tanh activation on the output to restrict generated images to be in the range -1 to 1.

Now that the models are defined, we can look at the loss functions that the GAN will need in order to train.

GAN loss function

As mentioned earlier, both the discriminator and generator have their own loss functions that depend on the output of each others networks. We can think of the GAN as playing a minimax game between the discriminator and the generator that looks like the following:

$$\min_{G} \max_{D} V(D, G) = \mathop{\mathbb{E}}_{x \sim p_{data}(x)} \left[\log D(x)\right] + \mathop{\mathbb{E}}_{z \sim p_z(z)} \left[\log(1 - D(G(z)))\right]$$

Here, D is our discriminator, G is our generator, z is a random vector input to the generator, and x is a real image. Although we have given the combined GAN loss here, it is actually easier to consider the two optimizations separately.

In order to train the GAN, we will alternate gradient step updates between the discriminator and the generator. When updating the discriminator, we want to try and **maximize** the probability that the discriminator makes the **right choice**. When updating the generator, we want to try and **minimize** the probability that the discriminator makes the **right choice**.

However, for practical implementation, we will alter the GAN loss function slightly from what we gave earlier; this is done to help training converge. The alterations are that when updating the generator, rather than **minimize** the probability that the discriminator makes the **right choice**; we instead **maximize** the probability that the discriminator makes the **wrong choice**:

$$\underset{G}{\text{maximize}} \; \mathbb{E}_{z \sim p(z)}[\log D(G(z))]$$

When updating the discriminator, we try to **maximize** the probability that it makes the correct choice on both real and fake data:

$$\underset{D}{\text{maximize}} \; \mathbb{E}_{x \sim p_{\text{data}}}[\log D(x)] + \mathbb{E}_{z \sim p(z)}[\log(1 - D(G(z)))]$$

Generator loss

The generator wants to fool the discriminator, in other words, make the discriminator output *1* for a generated image *G(z)* . The generator loss is just the negative of the binomial cross entropy loss applied to the discriminator output of a result from the generator. Note that as the generator is always trying to generate "real" images, the cross entropy loss simplifies down to this:

$$\frac{1}{m} \sum_{i=1}^{m} log(D(G(z^i)))$$

Here, each term means as follows:

- **m**: Batch size
- **D**: Discriminator
- **G**: Generator
- **z**: Random noise vector

We want to maximize this loss function when training our GAN. When the loss is maximized, it means the generator is capable of generating images that can fool the discriminator, and the discriminator is outputting 1 for generated images.

Discriminator loss

The discriminator wants to be able to distinguish between real and generated images. It wants to output 1 for real image and 0 for generated images. The discriminator loss function has the following formula, again simplified because of the way GAN training and labeling works:

$$\frac{1}{m} \sum_{i=1}^{m} [logD(x^i) + log(1 - D(G(z^i)))]$$

This loss function has two terms to it:

- Binomial cross entropy applied to the discriminator model results in some real data x
- Binomial cross entropy applied to the discriminator model result for generated data, $G(z)$

As earlier, we take the negative of these and want to maximize this loss function when training our GAN. When this loss is maximized, it means the discriminator is capable of distinguishing between real and generated outputs. Note that this loss is maximized when the discriminator outputs 1 for real images and 0 for generated images.

Putting the losses together

In TensorFlow, we can implement the whole GAN loss, as shown in the following code. As input, we take the output of the discriminator for a batch of fake images from the generator and a batch of real images from our dataset:

```
def gan_loss(logits_real, logits_fake):
    # Target label vectors for generator and discriminator losses.
    true_labels = tf.ones_like(logits_real)
    fake_labels = tf.zeros_like(logits_fake)
    # DISCRIMINATOR loss has 2 parts: how well it classifies real images
and how well it
    # classifies fake images.
    real_image_loss =
tf.nn.sigmoid_cross_entropy_with_logits(logits=logits_real,
labels=true_labels)
    fake_image_loss =
tf.nn.sigmoid_cross_entropy_with_logits(logits=logits_fake,
labels=fake_labels)
```

```
    # Combine and average losses over the batch
    discriminator_loss = tf.reduce_mean(real_image_loss + fake_image_loss)

    # GENERATOR is trying to make the discriminator output 1 for all its
images.
    # So we use our target label vector of ones for computing generator
loss.
    generator_loss =
tf.nn.sigmoid_cross_entropy_with_logits(logits=logits_fake,
labels=true_labels)

    # Average generator loss over the batch.
    generator_loss = tf.reduce_mean(G_loss)

    return discriminator_loss , generator_loss
```

You probably noted that it is impossible to maximize both discriminator loss and the generator loss at the same time. This is the beauty of the GAN, as when it trains, the model will hopefully reach some equilibrium, where the generator is having to produce really good quality images in order to fool the discriminator.

> TensorFlow only allows its optimizers to minimize and not maximize. As a result, we actually take the negative of the loss functions described earlier, which means we go from maximizing them to minimizing them. We don't have to do anything extra though, as `tf.nn.sigmoid_cross_entropy_with_logits()` takes care of this for us.

Training the GAN

So now that we have a generator, a discriminator, and our loss function, all that is left is to train! We will give a sketch idea of how to do this in TensorFlow, because there is nothing fancy in this part; it is just piecing together the stuff from the previous section, along with loading and feeding MNIST images, as we did earlier.

First, set up two solvers: one for the discriminator and one for the generator. A smaller value of `beta1` for the `AdamOptimizer` is used as it has been shown to help GAN train to converge:

```
    discriminator_solver = tf.train.AdamOptimizer(learning_rate=0.001,
    beta1=0.5)
    generator_solver = tf.train.AdamOptimizer(learning_rate=0.001, beta1=0.5)
```

Next, create a random noise vector; this can be done with `tf.random_uniform`. This is fed to the generator network to create a batch of generated images:

```
z = tf.random_uniform(maxval=1,minval=-1,shape=[batch_size, dim])
generator_sample = generator(z)
```

Then, we feed a batch of real images and our batch of generated samples to the discriminator. We use variable scope here to reuse our model variables and ensure that a second graph isn't created:

```
with tf.variable_scope("") as scope:
    logits_real = discriminator(x)
    # We want to re-use the discriminator weights.
    scope.reuse_variables()
    logits_fake = discriminator(generator_sample )
```

We separate the weights belonging to the discriminator and the generator, as we need to update them separately:

```
discriminator_vars = tf.get_collection(tf.GraphKeys.TRAINABLE_VARIABLES,
'discriminator')
generator_vars = tf.get_collection(tf.GraphKeys.TRAINABLE_VARIABLES,
'generator')
```

Finally, we calculate our losses and send them to our optimizers with the relevant weights to update:

```
discriminator_loss, generator_loss = gan_loss(logits_real, logits_fake)

# Training steps.
discriminator_train_step =
discriminator_solver.minimize(discriminator_loss,
var_list=discriminator_vars )
generator_train_step = generator_solver.minimize(generator_loss ,
var_list=generator_vars )
```

These are the main steps to training a GAN. All that is left is to create a training loop, iterating over batches of data. If you do this, you should be able to feed in any random noise vector, like we did in training, and generate an image.

As you can see in the following diagram, the images created are starting to resemble MNIST digits:

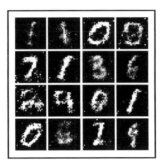

Deep convolutional GAN

Deep Convolutional GAN (DCGAN) is an extension of the normal GAN that we saw previously. Rather than using fully connected layers, we work with convolution layers. The idea is that the use of convolution layers helps the generator form better images. Here's what an example of this kind of model might look like:

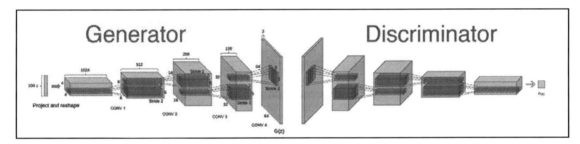

An example implementation of DCGAN would be the same as training a normal GAN, as earlier, but simply swapping out the discriminator and generator networks for some convolutional architectures, like in the following code. Note that the generator will make use of transposed convolutions to upsample:

```
def discriminator(x):
        with tf.variable_scope("discriminator"):
        unflatten = tf.reshape(x, shape=[-1, 28, 28, 1])
        conv1 = tf.layers.conv2d(inputs=unflatten, kernel_size=5,
strides=1, filters=32 ,activation=leaky_relu)
        maxpool1 = tf.layers.max_pooling2d(inputs=conv1, pool_size=2,
strides=2)
        conv2 = tf.layers.conv2d(inputs=maxpool1, kernel_size=5,
```

```
strides=1, filters=64,activation=leaky_relu)
        maxpool2 = tf.layers.max_pooling2d(inputs=conv2, pool_size=2,
strides=2)
        flatten = tf.reshape(maxpool2, shape=[-1, 1024])
        fc1 = tf.layers.dense(inputs=flatten, units=1024,
activation=leaky_relu)
        logits = tf.layers.dense(inputs=fc1, units=1)
        return logits

def generator(z):
    with tf.variable_scope("generator"):
        fc1 = tf.layers.dense(inputs=z, units=1024, activation=tf.nn.relu)
        bn1 = tf.layers.batch_normalization(inputs=fc1, training=True)
        fc2 = tf.layers.dense(inputs=bn1, units=7*7*128,
activation=tf.nn.relu)
        bn2 = tf.layers.batch_normalization(inputs=fc2, training=True)
        reshaped = tf.reshape(bn2, shape=[-1, 7, 7, 128])
        conv_transpose1 = tf.layers.conv2d_transpose(inputs=reshaped,
filters=64, kernel_size=4, strides=2, activation=tf.nn.relu,
                                             padding='same')
        bn3 = tf.layers.batch_normalization(inputs=conv_transpose1,
training=True)
        conv_transpose2 = tf.layers.conv2d_transpose(inputs=bn3,
filters=1, kernel_size=4, strides=2, activation=tf.nn.tanh,
                                             padding='same')

        img = tf.reshape(conv_transpose2, shape=[-1, 784])
        return img
```

Just by swapping out the generator and discriminator networks to use convolution operations, we are able to generate images like the following one:

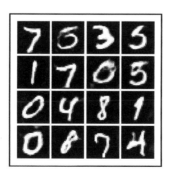

The quality produced is now extremely good and nearly indistinguishable from the real data. Also, note that the images are really sharp, and there is no blurring and little artifacts, like we had earlier.

Some points to pay attention to are these:

- For the discriminator: Use leaky relu again, don't use max pooling. Only use strided convolution or average pooling.
- For the generator: Use relu and tanh on the last layer.
- Generally, the best practice is to use batchnorm layers on both generator and discriminator . They will be set to training mode all the time.
- Sometimes, people run the generator optimizer twice as many times as running the discriminator optimizer.

Here's an example of the kind of quality that a simple DCGAN can achieve when tasked with generating images of faces:

WGAN

Wasserstein GAN is another variant of GANs that solve an issue that can happen when training GANs, called mode collapse. Moreover, it aims to give a metric that indicates when the GAN has converged, in other words, a loss function where the value has a meaning.

Important changes are to remove log from loss and clip the discriminator weights.

Also, follow these steps:

- Train discriminator more than generator
- Clip the weights of discriminator
- Use RMSProp instead of Adam
- Use low learning rates (0.0005)

A disadvantage of WGANs is that they are slower to train :

```
""" Vanilla GAN """
D_loss = -tf.reduce_mean(tf.log(D_real) + tf.log(1. - D_fake))
G_loss = -tf.reduce_mean(tf.log(D_fake))

""" WGAN """
D_loss = tf.reduce_mean(D_real) - tf.reduce_mean(D_fake)
G_loss = -tf.reduce_mean(D_fake)
```

```
""" Vanilla GAN """
def discriminator(x):
    D_h1 = tf.nn.relu(tf.matmul(x, D_W1) + D_b1)
    out = tf.matmul(D_h1, D_W2) + D_b2
    return tf.nn.sigmoid(out)

""" WGAN """
def discriminator(x):
    D_h1 = tf.nn.relu(tf.matmul(x, D_W1) + D_b1)
    out = tf.matmul(D_h1, D_W2) + D_b2
    return out
```

```
# theta_D is list of D's params
clip_D = [p.assign(tf.clip_by_value(p, -0.01, 0.01)) for p in theta_D]
```

The image results produced by WGAN are still not that great, but this model does manage to help solve the mode collapse issue.

BEGAN

The main idea of BEGAN is to use an autoencoder on the discriminator, which will have its own loss that measures how well the autoencoder reconstructed some image (generator or real data):

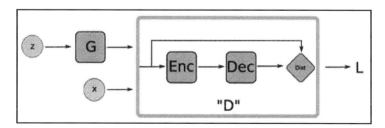

Some advantages of BEGAN are as listed:

- High-resolution (128x128) face generation (2017 state of the art) .
- Offers a way to measure convergence .
- Good results even without batch-norm and dropout .
- Hyperparameter to control the generation diversity versus quality. More quality also means more mode collapse.
- Having two separate optimizers are not required .

Here's an example of the quality of images that a BEGAN can produce when tasked with generating human faces:

Conditional GANs

Conditional GANs are an extension of the normal GANs, where both the discriminator and the generator are conditioned to some specific class y. This has interesting applications, because you can fix your generator to a specific class and then make it produce multiple different versions of a specific same class of our choosing. For example, if you set y to be the label corresponding to the digit 7 in MNIST, the generator will only produce images of sevens.

With conditional GANs, the minimax game becomes the following:

$$\min_{G} \max_{D} V(D, G) = \mathbb{E}_{x \sim p_{data}(x)} \left[\log D(x, y)\right] + \mathbb{E}_{z \sim p_z(z)} \left[\log(1 - D(G(z, y), y))\right]$$

Here, we depend on the extra input y, which is the class label of the input image.

The simplest way to merge x and y, or z and y, is to just concatenate them together so that our input vector is longer. This creates a much more controlled dataset augmentation system. Here's an example of this in TensorFlow code:

```python
def generator(z, y):
    # Concatenate z and y
    inputs = tf.concat(concat_dim=1, values=[z, y])

    G_h1 = tf.nn.relu(tf.matmul(inputs, G_W1) + G_b1)
    G_log_prob = tf.matmul(G_h1, G_W2) + G_b2
    G_prob = tf.nn.sigmoid(G_log_prob)

    return G_prob


def discriminator(x, y):
    # Concatenate x and y
    inputs = tf.concat(concat_dim=1, values=[x, y])

    D_h1 = tf.nn.relu(tf.matmul(inputs, D_W1) + D_b1)
    D_logit = tf.matmul(D_h1, D_W2) + D_b2
    D_prob = tf.nn.sigmoid(D_logit)

    return D_prob, D_logit
```

Problems with GANs

The current biggest problem with GANs is that they are very tricky to train. Luckily, there are some techniques that help make things easier, and it is a very active area of research at the moment.

Here, we will present some of the problems with training GANs and how to address them.

Loss interpretability

One of the problems while training GANs is that the values of both the generator and discriminator loss do not have a noticeable effect. It's not like training a classifier that you just wait for the loss to drop to see whether your model is training.

With GANs, the loss values' dropping does not necessarily mean that the model is training:

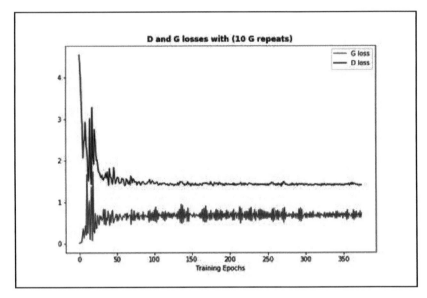

From many people's experiments and research, here are some tips on how to use the GAN loss values:

- You don't want that the discriminator loss to go down really fast, because it will not be able to provide feedback to the generator to improve it.
- If the generator loss falls quickly, it means that it found a single discriminator weakness and is exploiting this weakness again and again. If this happens, it is called **mode collapse**.

The loss is really only good for seeing if something has gone wrong in training. Consequently, there is no good way of knowing that training has converged. Normally, what is best to do is to keep looking at the output of generator. Ensure that the outputs are looking close to what you expect and that there is good variety in them.

Mode collapse

This is likely to be the first problem that you encounter when training GANs. Mode collapse happens when the generator finds a particular set of inputs able to fool the discriminator, and it keeps exploiting this failure case and collapsing lots of values from the latent Z space to the same value.

One solution for this problem is to use "Minibatches-features" or "Unrolled Gans", or just stop training entirely and start again when the generator starts to create a very narrow distribution of outputs:

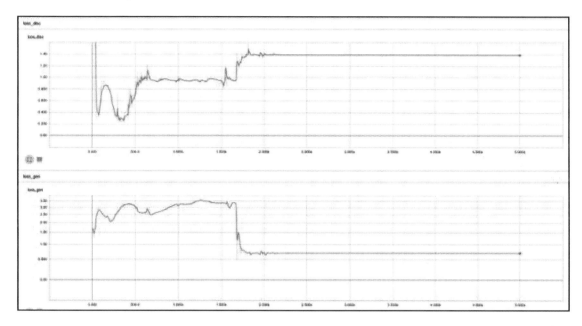

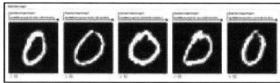

Techniques to improve GANs' trainability

Here, we will describe some techniques to make life easier when training GANs:

- Normalize inputs between -1/1
- Use BatchNorm
- Use Leaky Relu (discriminator)
- Use Relu (Generator), tanh on generator output
- For downsampling use average pooling or strided convolution
- Use Adam optimizer

- If Discriminator loss went down fast, something is wrong
- Use dropout on generator (both train and test phase)

Minibatch discriminator

Some techniques used to improve mode collapse are as follows:

- Take the output of some layer of the discriminator
- Reshape the input of the discriminator to a matrix
- Compute the L1 distance
- Calculate the sum of the exponentials of the L1 distances
- Concatenate results to the input (some layer of discriminator)

```
# Minibatch feature
# https://arxiv.org/pdf/1606.03498.pdf
def minibatch(input, num_kernels=5, kernel_dim=3):
    # Transform feature into a matrix
    x = linear(input, num_kernels * kernel_dim)
    activation = tf.reshape(x, (-1, num_kernels, kernel_dim))

    # Calculate the L1 and then the sum of the negative exponential
    diffs = tf.expand_dims(activation, 3) - tf.expand_dims(tf.transpose(activation, [1, 2, 0]), 0)
    abs_diffs = tf.reduce_sum(tf.abs(diffs), 2)
    minibatch_features = tf.reduce_sum(tf.exp(-abs_diffs), 2)

    # Concatenate results back on the input (of some layer of the discriminator)
    return tf.concat(1, [input, minibatch_features])
```

```
def discriminator_mb(input, h_dim):
    h0 = util.lrelu(util.linear_std(input, hidden_size * 2, 'd0'))
    h1 = util.lrelu(util.linear_std(h0, hidden_size * 2, 'd1'))
    # Notice that using the mini-batch technique the discriminator can be smaller
    h2 = minibatch(h1)
    h3 = tf.sigmoid(util.linear_std(h2, 1, 'd3'))
    return h3
```

Summary

In this chapter, we learned about generative models and what makes them different from discriminative models. We also discussed the different kinds of autoencoders, including deep, variational, and convolutional. In addition, we learned about a new type of generative model, called a generative adversarial network (GAN). After learning about all these generative models, we saw how we could train them ourselves in TensorFlow for generating handwritten digits and saw the different quality images that they can each produce.

In Chapter 7, *Transfer Learning*, we will learn about transfer learning and how it can help us speed up training.

Transfer Learning 7

Transfer learning does exactly as the name says. The idea is to transfer something learned from one task and apply it to another. Why? Practically speaking, training entire models from scratch every time is inefficient, and its success depends on many factors. Another important reason is that for certain applications, the datasets that are publicly available are not big enough to train a deep architecture like AlexNet or ResNet without over-fitting, which means failing to generalize. Example applications could be online learning from a few examples given by the user or fine-grained classification, where the variation between the classes is minimal.

A very interesting observation is that final layers can be used to work on different tasks, given that you freeze all the rest, whether it be detection or classification, end up having weights that look very similar.

This leads to the idea of transfer learning. This means a deep architecture that is trained on a significantly large amount of data (for example, ImageNet) can generalize so well that its convolutional weights can act as feature extractors, similar to conventional visual representations and can be used to train a linear classifier for various tasks.

This chapter aims to teach the reader how to take readily available trained models, change their structure, and retrain certain layers for specific tasks in TensorFlow. We will see how transfer learning will help improve results and speed up training time.

The main topics covered in this chapter are as follows:

- Pre-initializing a model with weights from another trained model
- Using TensorFlow to load the models and freeze/unfreeze layers when needed

When?

Research has shown that feature extraction in convolutional network weights trained on ImageNet outperforms the conventional feature extraction methods such as SURF, **Deformable Part Descriptors (DPDs)**, **Histogram of Oriented Gradients (HOG)**, and **bag of words (BoW)**. This means that convolutional features can be used equally well wherever the conventional visual representations work, with the only drawback being that deeper architectures might require a longer time to extract the features.

When a deep convolutional neural network is trained on ImageNet the visualization of convolution filters in the first layers (refer to the following illustration) shows that they learn *low-level* features similar to edge detection filters, while the convolution filters at the last layers learn *high-level* features that capture the class-specific information. Hence, if we extract the features for ImageNet after the first pooling layer and embed them into a 2D space (using, for example, t-SNE), the visualization will show that there is some anarchy in the data, while if we do the same at fully connected layers, we will notice that the data with the same semantic information gets organized into clusters. This implies that the network generalizes quite well at higher levels, and it will be possible to transfer this knowledge to unseen classes.

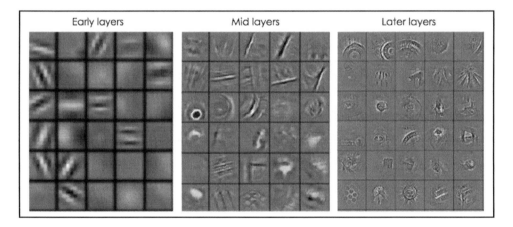

According to experiments conducted on datasets with a small degree of similarity with respect to ImageNet, the features based on convolutional neural network weights trained on ImageNet perform better than the conventional feature extraction methods for the following tasks:

- **Object recognition**: This CNN feature extractor can successfully perform classification tasks on other datasets with unseen classes.
- **Domain adaptation**: This is when the training and testing data are from different distributions, while the labels and number of classes are the same. Different domains can consider images captured with different devices or in different settings and environment conditions. A linear classifier with CNN features successfully clusters images with the same semantic information across different domains, while SURF features overfit to domain-specific characteristics.
- **Fine-grained classification**: This is when we want to classify between the subcategories within the same high-level class. For example, we can categorize between bird species. CNN features, along with logistic regression, although not trained on fine-grained data, perform better than the baseline approaches.
- **Scene recognition**: Here, we need to classify the scene of the entire image. A CNN feature extractor trained on object classification databases with a simple linear classifier on top, outperforms complex learning algorithms applied on traditional feature extractors on recognition data.

Some of the tasks mentioned here are not directly related to image classification, which was the primary goal while training on ImageNet and therefore someone would expect that the CNN features would fail to generalize to unseen scenarios. However, those features, combined with a simple linear classifier, outperform the hand-crafted features. This means that the learned weights of a CNN are reusable.

So when should we use transfer learning? When we have a task where the available dataset is small due to the nature of the problem (such as classify ants/bees). In this case, we can train our model on a larger dataset that contains similar semantic information and subsequently, retrain the last layer only (linear classifier) with the small dataset. If we have just enough data available, and there is a larger similar dataset to ours, pretraining on this similar dataset may result in a more robust model. As normally we train models with the weights randomly initialized, in this case, they will be initialized with the weights trained on this other dataset. This will facilitate the network to converge faster and generalise better. In this scenario, it would make sense to only fine-tune a few layers at the top end of the model.

Rule of thumb is that the more data you have available, the more layers you can train, starting from the top of the network. Initialize your model weights from a pre-trained, for example, on ImageNet, model.

How? An overview

How should we use transfer learning? There are two typical ways to go about this. The first and less timely way, is to use what is known as a pre-trained model, that is, a model that has previously been trained on a large scale dataset, for example, the ImageNet dataset. These pre-trained models are readily available across different deep learning frameworks and are often referred to as "model zoos". The choice of a pre-trained model is largely dependent on what the current task to be solved is, and on the size of the datasets. After the choice of model, we can use all of it or parts of it, as the initialized model for the actual task that we want to solve.

The other, less common way deep learning is to pretrain the model ourselves. This typically occurs when the available pretrained networks are not suitable to solve specific problems, and we have to design the network architecture ourselves. Obviously, this requires more time and effort to design the model and prepare the dataset. In some cases, the dataset to pretrain the network on can even be synthetic, generated from computer graphics engines such as 3D studio Max or Unity, or other convolutional neural networks, such as GANs. The model pretrained on virtual data can be fine-tuned on real data, and it can work equally well with a model trained solely on real data.

If, for example, we want to discriminate between cats and dogs, and we do not have enough data, we can download a network trained on ImageNet from the "model zoo" and use the weights from all but the last of its layers. The last layer has to be adjusted to have the same size as the number of classes, in our case two, and the weights to be reinitialized and trained. In this way, we do what we call freezing of the layers that are not to be trained by setting the learning rate for these layers to zero, or to a very small number (refer to the following figure). In case a bigger dataset is available, we can train the last three fully connected layers. Sometimes, the pretrained network can be used only to initialize the weights and then be trained normally.

Transfer learning works because the features computed at the initial layers are more general and look similar. The features extracted in the top layers become more specific to the problem that we want to solve.

For a further look into how to use transfer learning, and a deeper understanding of the topic, let's take a look at the code.

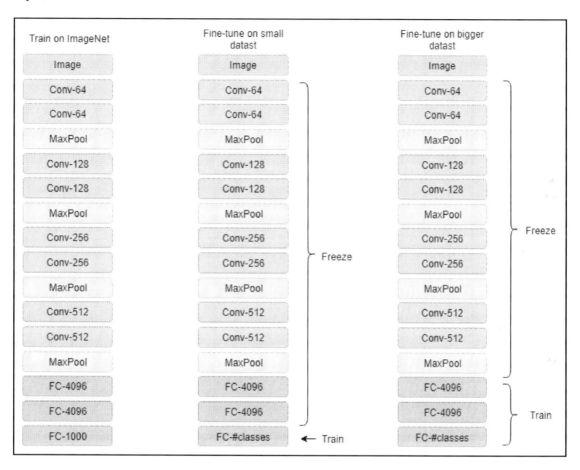

How? Code example

In this section we will learn the practical skills needed to perform transfer learning in TensorFlow. More specifically, we will learn how to select layers to be loaded from a checkpoint and also how to instruct our solver to optimize only specific layers while freezing the others.

TensorFlow useful elements

Since transfer learning is about training a network initialized with weights taken from another trained model, we will need to find one. In our example, we will use the encoding part of a pretrained convolutional autoencoder that was explained in chapter 6. The advantage of using an autoencoder is that we do not need labelled data, that is, it can be trained completely unsupervised.

An autoencoder without the decoder

An encoder (autoencoder without the decoder part) that consists of two convolutional layers and one fully connected layer is presented as follows. The parent autoencoder was trained on the MNIST dataset. Therefore, the network takes as input an image of size 28x28x1 and at latent space, encodes it to a 10-dimensional vector, one dimension for each class:

```
# Only half of the autoencoder changed for classification
class CAE_CNN_Encoder(object):
    ......
    def build_graph(self, img_size=28):
        self.__x = tf.placeholder(tf.float32, shape=[None, img_size *
img_size], name='IMAGE_IN')
        self.__x_image = tf.reshape(self.__x, [-1, img_size, img_size, 1])
        self.__y_ = tf.placeholder("float", shape=[None, 10], name='Y')

        with tf.name_scope('ENCODER'):
            ##### ENCODER
            # CONV1: Input 28x28x1 after CONV 5x5 P:2 S:2 H_out: 1 +
(28+4-5)/2 = 14,
            # W_out= 1 + (28+4-5)/2 = 14
            self.__conv1_act = tf.layers.conv2d(inputs=self.__x_image,
strides=(2, 2), name='conv1',
                                filters=16, kernel_size=[5, 5],
padding="same", activation=tf.nn.relu)

            # CONV2: Input 14x14x16 after CONV 5x5 P:0 S:2 H_out: 1 +
```

```
(14+4-5)/2 = 7,
            # W_out= 1 + (14+4-5)/2 = 7
            self.__conv2_act = tf.layers.conv2d(inputs=self.__conv1_act,
strides=(2, 2),
                name='conv2', filters=32, kernel_size=[5, 5],
padding="same", activation=tf.nn.relu)

        with tf.name_scope('LATENT'):
            # Reshape: Input 7x7x32 after [7x7x32]
            self.__enc_out = tf.layers.flatten(self.__conv2_act,
name='flatten_conv2')
            self.__dense = tf.layers.dense(inputs=self.__enc_out,
units=200, activation=tf.nn.relu,
name='fc1')
            self.__logits = tf.layers.dense(inputs=self.__dense, units=10,
name='logits')

    def __init__(self, img_size=28):
        if CAE_CNN_Encoder.__instance is None:
            self.build_graph(img_size)

    @property
    def output(self):
        return self.__logits

    @property
    def labels(self):
        return self.__y_

    @property
    def input(self):
        return self.__x

    @property
    def image_in(self):
        return self.__x_image
```

Selecting layers

Once the model is defined, `model = CAE_CNN_Encoder()`, it is important to select layers that will be initialized with pretrained weights. Pay attention that the structure of both networks, the one to be initialized and the one that gives the trained weights, must be the same. So, for example, the following snippet of code will select all layers with name `convs` of `fc`:

```
from models import CAE_CNN_Encoder
model = CAE_CNN_Encoder()

list_convs = [v for v in tf.global_variables() if "conv" in v.name]
list_fc_linear = [v for v in tf.global_variables() if "fc" in v.name or
"output" in v.name]
```

Note that those lists are populated from `tf.global_variables()`; if we choose to print its content, we might observe that it holds all the model variables as shown:

```
[<tf.Variable 'conv1/kernel:0' shape=(5, 5, 1, 16) dtype=float32_ref>,
 <tf.Variable 'conv1/bias:0' shape=(16,) dtype=float32_ref>,
 <tf.Variable 'conv2/kernel:0' shape=(5, 5, 16, 32) dtype=float32_ref>,
 <tf.Variable 'conv2/bias:0' shape=(32,) dtype=float32_ref>,
 <tf.Variable 'fc1/kernel:0' shape=(1568, 200) dtype=float32_ref>,
 <tf.Variable 'fc1/bias:0' shape=(200,) dtype=float32_ref>,
 <tf.Variable 'logits/kernel:0' shape=(200, 10) dtype=float32_ref>,
 <tf.Variable 'logits/bias:0' shape=(10,) dtype=float32_ref>]
```

Once the layers of the defined graph are grouped into two lists, convolutional and fully connected, you will use `tf.Train.Saver` to load the weights that you prefer. First we need to create a saver object, giving as input the list of variables that we want to load from a checkpoint as follows:

```
# Define the saver object to load only the conv variables
saver_load_autoencoder = tf.train.Saver(var_list=list_convs)
```

In addition to `saver_load_autoencoder` we need to create another `saver` object that will allow us to store all the variables of the network to be trained into checkpoints.

```
# Define saver object to save all the variables during training
saver = tf.train.Saver()
```

Then, after the graph is initialized with `init = tf.global_variables_initializer()` and a session is created, we can use `saver_load_autoencoder` to restore the convolutional layers from a checkpoint as follows:

```
# Restore only the weights (From AutoEncoder)
  saver_load_autoencoder.restore(sess, "../tmp/cae_cnn/model.ckpt-34")
```

Note that calling `restore` overrides the `global_variables_initializer` an all the selected weights are replaced by the ones from the checkpoint.

Training only some layers

Another important part of transfer learning is freezing the weights of the layers that you don't want to train, while allowing some layers (typically the final ones) to be trained. In TensorFlow, we can pass to our solver only the layers that we want to optimize (in this example, only the FC layers):

```
train_step = tf.train.AdamOptimizer(learning_rate).minimize(loss,
var_list=list_fc_linear)
```

Complete source

In this example, we will load the weights from a MNIST convolutional autoencoder example. We will restore the weights of the encoder part only, freeze the CONV layers, and train the FC layers to perform digits classification:

```
import tensorflow as tf
import numpy as np
import os
from models import CAE_CNN_Encoder
SAVE_FOLDER='/tmp/cae_cnn_transfer'
from tensorflow.examples.tutorials.mnist import input_data
mnist = input_data.read_data_sets("MNIST_data/", one_hot=True)
model = CAE_CNN_Encoder(latent_size = 20)
model_in = model.input
model_out = model.output
labels_in = model.labels

# Get all convs weights
list_convs = [v for v in tf.global_variables() if "conv" in v.name]

# Get fc1 and logits
list_fc_layers = [v for v in tf.global_variables() if "fc" in v.name or
```

```
"logits" in v.name]

# Define the saver object to load only the conv variables
saver_load_autoencoder = tf.train.Saver(var_list=list_convs)

# Define saver object to save all the variables during training
saver = tf.train.Saver()

# Define loss for classification
with tf.name_scope("LOSS"):
    loss =
tf.reduce_mean(tf.nn.softmax_cross_entropy_with_logits_v2(logits=model_out,
labels=labels_in))
correct_prediction = tf.equal(tf.argmax(model_out,1),
tf.argmax(labels_in,1))
accuracy = tf.reduce_mean(tf.cast(correct_prediction, tf.float32))

# Solver configuration
with tf.name_scope("Solver"):
    train_step = tf.train.AdamOptimizer(1e-4).minimize(loss,
var_list=list_fc_layers)

# Initialize variables
init = tf.global_variables_initializer()

# Avoid allocating the whole memory
gpu_options = tf.GPUOptions(per_process_gpu_memory_fraction=0.200)
sess = tf.Session(config=tf.ConfigProto(gpu_options=gpu_options))

sess.run(init)

# Restore only the CONV weights (From AutoEncoder)
saver_load_autoencoder.restore(sess, "/tmp/cae_cnn/model.ckpt-34")

# Add some tensors to observe on tensorboad
tf.summary.image("input_image", model.image_in, 4)
tf.summary.scalar("loss", loss)

merged_summary = tf.summary.merge_all()
writer = tf.summary.FileWriter(SAVE_FOLDER)
writer.add_graph(sess.graph)

#####Train######
num_epoch = 200
batch_size = 10
for epoch in range(num_epoch):
    for i in range(int(mnist.train.num_examples / batch_size)):
        # Get batch of 50 images
```

```
        batch = mnist.train.next_batch(batch_size)

        # Dump summary
        if i % 5000 == 0:
            # Other summaries
            s = sess.run(merged_summary, feed_dict={model_in:batch[0],
labels_in:batch[1]})
            writer.add_summary(s,i)

        # Train actually here (Also get loss value)
        _, val_loss, t_acc = sess.run((train_step, loss, accuracy),
feed_dict={model_in:batch[0],
labels_in:batch[1]})

    print('Epoch: %d/%d loss:%d' % (epoch, num_epoch, val_loss))
    print('Save model:', epoch)
    saver.save(sess, os.path.join(SAVE_FOLDER, "model.ckpt"), epoch)
```

Summary

In this chapter, we learned how, when, and why to use transfer learning. This is considered to be a very powerful tool, because it allows us to generalize well with less data using features learned from other domains. We looked at some examples, and it should now be clear how to implement transfer learning in your own tasks.

In the next chapter, we will see how to organize our data and how to scale the CNN architectures in order to build accurate and practical machine learning systems.

8
Machine Learning Best Practices and Troubleshooting

It is essential in machine learning engineering to know how to proceed during the development of a system to avoid pitfalls and address common issues. The easiest way to create a machine learning system, that saves you money and time, is to reuse code and pretrained models that have been applied to similar problems to your own. If this does not cover your needs, then you may need to train your own CNN architecture as this can sometimes be the best way to solve your problem. However, one of the biggest challenges to face is finding large scale, publicly available datasets that are tailor-made to your problem. Therefore, it is often the case that you may need to create your own dataset. When creating your own dataset it is very crucial to organize it appropriately in order to insure successful model training.

In this chapter we will present and discuss the day-to-day workflow that will help you to answer the following questions:

- How should I split my dataset?
- Is my dataset representative enough of my problem?
- How complex should my model be to be both efficient and accurate?
- What is the best method to evaluate my model?
- How should I structure my code?

Building Machine Learning Systems

In order to build a machine learning system, it is advised to start with a new small project and improve it progressively:

1. Find a similar problem to yours and download code (and test the model to check results)
2. Find ways to scale your computation if needed (namely, AWS/Google Cloud)
3. Start with smaller datasets to avoid losing time just waiting for a single epoch
4. Start with a simple architecture
5. Use visualization/debugging (for instance, TensorBoard)
6. Fine-tune the model, fine-tune hyperparameters, depth, architecture, layers, and the loss function
7. Expand your dataset and ensure that it is as clean as possible
8. Split your dataset into training, development, and testing sets
9. Evaluate your model

Data Preparation

The backbone of all Machine Learning algorithms is the data. Everything a machine learning algorithm learns is from the data. Therefore it is critical to provide the correct data to the algorithm which is representative of the problem statement. As seen already, deep learning in particular requires large amounts of data for training models. We can sometimes say that a certain amount of data is enough for a problem, however there is never enough! More is better. The complexity of the model that is able to be trained correctly is directly proportional to the amount of data on which it is trained. Limited data will put an upper limit on the choice of model architecture for the problem. When considering the amount of data available, it is also worth noting that a portion of this will also need to be used for validation and testing purposes.

The following section will now discuss the data partitioning and its importance on the progress of any machine learning task.

Split of Train/Development/Test set

Let us define the "Training Set", "Development Set" and "Test Set", before discussing the partitioning of the data into these.

- **Training set**: The set of data/examples used to train machine learning algorithm. In machine learning, this data is used to find the 'optimal' weights for the model/classifier. Typically, the majority of data used goes to the training set.
- **Development (dev)/validation set**: The portion of data which is used to evaluate the model/classifier at intermediate stages of training. This set is used to fine tune hyperparameters and evaluate model architecture with various configurations. It is used during the development of the model, not in the final model evaluation.
- **Test set**: Once the model is fine tuned and fully trained (we are happy with our loss on the training/dev sets), we consider it fully trained. This model is then evaluated. The data that this is evaluated on is called the test set. The test set consists of the unseen portion of the data, therefore providing an unbiased estimate of the final model performance.

In order to achieve a high performance neural network, it is very important to properly partition the dataset into training, development and test sets. It helps to iterate quicker. In addition, it allows to more efficiently measure the bias and variance of the algorithm so that we can select the ways to improve it in an efficient manner.

In previous eras when we had smaller datasets, say up to 10,000 examples, and simpler classifiers, we would split the dataset into a training and testing set. The training set would usually be split into smaller sets to train the classifier with a technique called cross-validation. It was also good practice to split the dataset at a ratio of 60/20/20 (i.e. 60% training data, 20% dev data, 20% test data). However, the modern era of Big Data has changed this rule of thumb. In cases where we have 1,000,000 examples, the ratio of split has changed to be 98/1/1 (i.e. 98% training data, 1% dev data, 1% test data).

The ratio of dev and test sets becomes smaller as we have even more data.

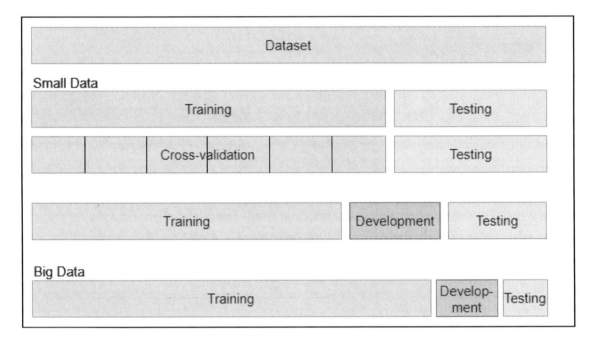

Mismatch of the Dev and Test set

In addition to the split of data, distribution of data has huge impact on the performance of a neural network. Most issues in applied deep learning come from the mismatch of the dev and test set data distribution. We need to bear in mind that the dev and test data should be coming from a similar distribution. For example, we will have a distribution mismatch if we collect and split person detection data in a way that training images of people are collected from web pages while test set images are collected using mobile phones. The problem here is that while training a model we finetune the parameters and architecture of a network based on its performance on the dev data, and if the dev data is similar to training data and different from test data then there is high bias in dev data towards the training set. Good evaluation results on the dev set do not necessarily mean that the model will generalize well. In this case, testing on a set with an entirely different distribution may evaluate to bad results. This is a waste of time and effort. The solution to this is to initially merge the dev and test sets, randomly shuffle them and finally split the shuffled data into dev and test sets again. This helps make faster progress in training machine learning algorithms successfully to your final application.

When to Change Dev/Test Set

An algorithm which performs well on the dev/test set according to evaluation metrics, but does not satisfy customer requirements (i.e. performs badly when deployed), indicates that we are missing the right target data in our dataset. In this situation we need to make changes to our dataset since it is not representative enough for the target application. Consider classification of cat images. If the train/dev/test set is using high resolution, good quality images (perfectly posed cats), while the target application is looking at the images which have cats from different viewpoints or that are in motion (blurry), we can expect our algorithm to perform badly when deployed.

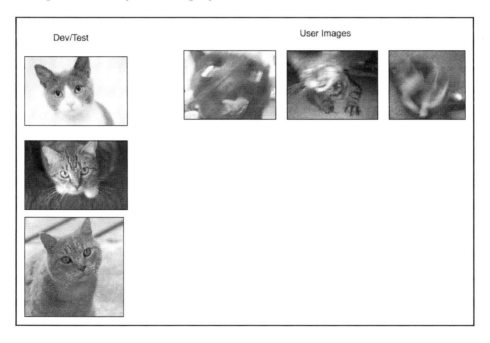

Bias and Variance

Variance and Bias is another way of saying overfitting and underfitting respectively, as discussed in `Chapter 2`, *Deep Learning and Convolutional Neural Networks*. We can diagnose the problem of "underfitting" and "overfitting" using the train set, dev set and test set errors.

Consider the following scenario where we have data coming from two different distributions named as Distribution 1 and Distribution 2. Distribution 2 represents the target application which we care about. The question is, how do we define train, dev and test sets on such distributions.

The best way to do so is to split it according to the preceding figure. Distribution 1 is split in to train set and part of it is used as the dev set. Here we are calling it the "Train-Dev set" (because the dev set has same distribution as train set). Distribution 1 is used mainly for training as it is a large dataset. Distribution 2 is split into test set and dev set which are independent of either sets from Distribution 1. One thing to emphasize here is that the test and dev set should be coming from the same distribution and belong to the application which we actually care about i.e. the target application. The dev and test sets are usually small datasets, as the purpose of these is to to give an unbiased performance estimate of the model/algorithm.

The difference in errors of the model on the different dataset partitions, and looking at the human level error can give us insight in diagnosing our problems of bias and variance

The following table shows what the diagnosis should be when there is a difference in error between the sets in the left column. N.B. Human level error is the benchmark in this analysis which gives a baseline to compare our model with.

Human level error	Bias		
Training error		Variance	
Train-dev error			Data mismatch	
Dev set error				Overfit dev set
Test set error				

This can be explained better by the following tables. In these examples, we assume optimal/human error in all cases to be minimal, that is, 1%. Normally, deep learning models have accuracy similar to humans, so having this as a comparison helps pave a path in finding a good architecture.

- High bias/underfitting

Human-level/optimal error	1%
Training error	15%

Having a high training error compared to human-level performance means that the model is not able to even fit the data; it is trained on and thus underfitting/high bias. However, when we look at the dev error in this case, it is generalizing well on it, so all is not lost.

- High variance/overfitting

Training error	1.5%
Train-dev error	30%

In this case, the model doesn't perform well on the unseen data, which belongs to the same distribution as the training set but is not part of training. This means that the model is not able to generalize and hence overfits the training data.

- High variance and high bias

Training error	20%
Train-dev error	40%

This situation is the worst case, as we observe that the model is not able to fit properly on the training data and also not generalizing well. This can be solved by changing the model architecture.

- Data mismatch

Train-dev error	2%
Dev error	15%

When the model is fitting well on the dev set coming from the same distribution as the training set and performs badly on the dev set coming from a different distribution, which leads to a data mismatch problem, as discussed earlier in the chapter.

- Overfit dev set

Dev error	2%
Test error	15%

The solution/guideline to address the mentioned problems is presented in the form of a flowchart in the following diagram:

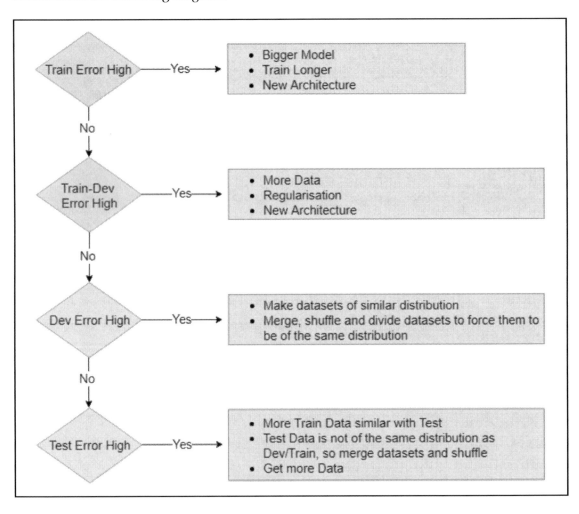

ML basic recipe

A useful graph that illustrates how the test and train error vary with model complexity is given as follows. On the one hand, when the model is too complex it tends to overfit to the training data, hence the Train Error decreases while Test Error increases. On the other hand a simpler model tends to underfit and fails to generalize. The ideal range for model complexity lies somewhere before the Test Error starts increasing and when the Train Error is approaching zero.

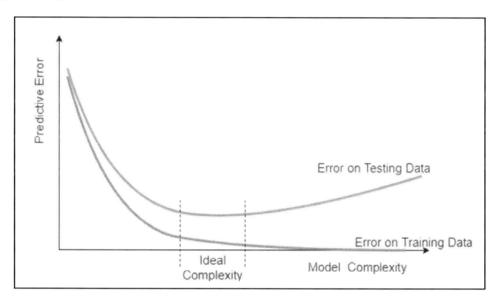

Data Imbalance

We have already seen the importance of data representation and distribution in tackling the problem of Bias and Variance. Another related problem we encounter is the unequal distribution of data among various classes in classification tasks. This is called data imbalance. For example if we have a binary classification problem and one of the classes has 50000 images and the other class has only 1000 images, this can lead to huge problems in the performance of the trained algorithm. We have to tackle this problem of imbalanced data by:

Collecting more data

Yes it is always better to make the class data distribution equal. Gather as much data as possible and populate the class with fewer samples. For this purpose you can search for databases over the internet which are similar to your problem and include these. Simple web searches can also bring many images uploaded by various sources. Sometimes you will see that the model performance does not improve with more data. This is an indication that your model might be at its limits.

Look at your performance metric

Classification accuracy is not a good measure, especially when we have imbalanced data. This accuracy will be more biased towards class with more data. There are many good performance evaluation metrics which provide a true picture of how an algorithm is performing such as the confusion matrix, Receiver **Operating Characteristic Curve**(ROC), **Precision Recall** (PR) curve and F1 score. These are explained in more detail later in this chapter.

Data synthesis/Augmentation

In situations where we can't collect data from other resources, datasets are too small, or the collected data is not well represented, we need to somehow generate data ourselves. This is called data augmentation. Smartly generated data can tackle many problems, including imbalanced datasets, not enough training data and overfitting.

Data augmentation is usually done as part of your input data pipeline that feeds your model while training. Randomly, instead of feeding an original training image, you will instead apply some augmentations to change it. There are many ways to do data augmentation but some examples are:

- Add noise
- Apply geometric transformations
- Swap color channels
- Random color perturbations
- Adjust brightness/contrast/hue

- simply add augmentations that are similar to what the network is having problems generalising to, for example, your model does not work for black and white images; simply add this as a new augmentation

Resample Data

This is about changing the way we build our training batch. We do this by changing the probability of selecting a certain class. For example if you have two classes, A and B, where we have much more instances of A than B, we could change our sampling system to select more B than A.

Loss function Weighting

We can also work with imbalanced classes and handle the classification problem for imbalanced data by including weights to the loss function. Such penalties or weights force model to focus more on the minority classes (class with fewer samples). Examples of this is penalized-SVM and Focal Loss detector algorithm discussed in previous chapters.

Tensorflow already has its loss functions with weighting options built-in:

- `tf.losses.sparse_softmax_cross_entropy(labels=label, logits=logits, weights=weights)`
- `Tf.nn.weighted_cross_entropy_with_logits`

For example, if you are trying to classify three classes A, B, C, where A is 10%, B is 45%, and C is 45%, you can use `tf.losses.sparse_softmax_cross_entropy` with the following weights: [1.0, 0.3, 0.3].

Evaluation Metrics

We also need to be careful when selecting the evaluation metrics for our model. Suppose that we have two algorithms with accuracies of 98% and 96% respectively, for a dog/not dog classification problem. At first glance the algorithms look like they both have similar performance. Let us remember that classification accuracy is defined as the number of correct predictions made divided by the total number of predictions made. In other words the number of True Positive (TP) and True Negative (TN) prediction, divided by the total number of predictions. However, it might be the case that along with dog images we are also getting large number of background or similar looking objects falsely classified as dogs, commonly known as false positives (FP). Another undesirable behavior could be that many dog images are misclassified as negatives or False Negative (FN). Clearly, by definition the classification accuracy does not capture the notion of false positives or false negatives. Therefore, better evaluation metrics are required.

As a first step what we would do is build a confusion matrix that summarizes the last paragraph as it is shown:

		Actual		Total
		Positive	Negative	
Predicted	Positive	True Positive (TP)	False Positive (FP)	TP+FP
	Negative	False Negative (FN)	True Negative (TN)	FN+TN
Total		TP+FN	FP+TN	

Based on this table we can define four additional metrics that will give us a better insight into the achieved results. These are:

- **True Positive Rate (TPR) or sensitivity or recall**: probability that a test result will be positive when the object is present (true positive rate, expressed as a percentage) = TP / (TP+FN)
- **False Positive rate (FPR)**: is the probability of falsely rejecting the actual negative for a particular test= FP / (FP+TN)
- **Positive predictive value (PPV) or precision**: probability that the object is present when the test is positive (expressed as a percentage) = TP / (TP+FP)

- **Negative predictive value (NPV)**: probability that the object is not present when the test is negative (expressed as a percentage) = TN / (TN+FN)

To understand better how these metrics are useful, let's take as an example the two following confusion matrices for two different algorithms and calculate the preceding metrics.

Example 1:

	Positive	Negative	
Predicted Positive	10 (TP)	13 (FP)	23
Predicted Negative	75 (FN)	188 (TN)	263
	85	201	286

Accuracy: (TP+TN)/(TP+TN+FP+FN)=198/286=0.69
TPR: TP / (TP+FN)= 10/85=0.11
FPR: FP /(FP+TN)= 13/201=0.06
PPV: TP/ (TP+FP)=10/23=0.43
NPV: TN / (TN+FN)= 188/263=0.71

Example 2:

	Positive	Negative	
Predicted Positive	0 (TP)	0 (FP)	0
Predicted Negative	85 (FN)	201 (TN)	286
	85	201	286

Accuracy: (TP+TN)/(TP+TN+FP+FN)=201/286=0.70
TPR: TP / (TP+FN)= 0/85=0
FPR: FP /(FP+TN)= 0/201=0
PPV: TP/ (TP+FP)=0/0=0
NPV: TN / (TN+FN)= 201/286=0.70

In the first example we get an okay accuracy of 69%, however in the second example, by just predicting negative for every example we actually increase our accuracy to 70%! Obviously a model that just predicts the negative class for everything isn't a great model and this is what we call the Accuracy Paradox. In simple terms, the Accuracy Paradox says that even though a model might have a higher accuracy it may not actually be a better model.

This phenomenon is more likely to happen when the class imbalance becomes large as in the preceding examples. The reader is encouraged to repeat the preceding test for a balanced dataset with 85 positive examples and 85 negative examples. If the proportion of false positives to true negatives remains the same as the preceding examples then this will lead to a classification accuracy of 52% for the 1st example and 50% for the 2nd example showing that the accuracy paradox does not hold for balanced datasets.

In order to be able to properly evaluate the algorithms we need to look at other evaluation metrics such as TPR and FPR. We can see that in the 2nd example they're both zero which shows that the algorithm cannot detect the desired positive object at all.

Another case of unbalanced datasets where the precision metric is useful is cancer tests where the number of sick are considerably less than the number of healthy. Following is a worked out example for this.

	Sick	Healthy	total
Test result positive	99 (TP)	999 (FP)	1,098
Test result negative	1(FN)	98,901(TN)	98,902
total	100	99,900	100,000

Accuracy: (TP+TN)/(TP+TN+FP+FN)=0.99
TPR: TP / (TP+FN)=0.99
FPR: FP /(FP+TN)= 0.01
PPV: TP/ (TP+FP)=0.09
NPV: TN / (TN+FN)= 0.99

The test here seems to perform reasonably well, as the accuracy is 99%. However if you are diagnosed with cancer this does not mean that the probability that you have the disease is 99%. It should be noted that only 99 out of 1098 that tested positive have the disease. This means that if you are given a positive test the probability that you actually have the disease is only 9% for a test that is 99% accurate.

These examples are a good warning that the aim should be to have a balanced split in your test data, especially if you are using the accuracy metric to compare effectiveness of different models.

Other useful means to compare different algorithms are the precision-recall and receiver-operating characteristic curves. These can be plotted if we calculate the preceding metrics for different threshold values. If the output of our algorithm is not binary (0 for negative and 1 for positive) but instead a score that approaches 1 when the test is positive and zero when the test is negative then the number of TP, TN, FP, FN will depend on the threshold value that we have selected.

Let's take the example of cat detection in images. For every region the classifier outputs a score which shows how confident it is about the detection. If we set a threshold of 0.5 then a score of 0.6 would show a positive detection while a score of 0.45 a negative one. If the threshold is lowered to 0.4, both detections become positive. The following table illustrates the preceding metrics varying with the threshold value.

Threshold	FPR	TPR	PPV	TP	TN	FN	FP
0.72	1	0.98	0.33	487	0	7	990
0.88	0.5	0.97	0.46	485	430	9	560
0.97	0.1	0.94	0.8	464	878	30	112
0.99	0.05	0.93	0.87	460	923	34	67
1.06	0.01	0.87	0.96	430	976	64	14
1.08	0.005	0.84	0.98	416	985	78	5
1.16	0.001	0.69	0.99	344	989	150	1

If we plot the FPR against the TPR, we will get what we call a ROC (Receiver Operator Characteristic) curve as shown:

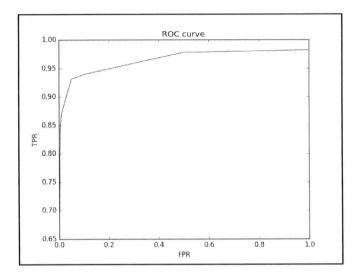

To get a Precision-Recall (PR) curve, we need to plot recall/TPR against precision/PPV. An example of the curve is shown in the following graph. The reader is advised to investigate further on how to interpret the ROC and PR curves.

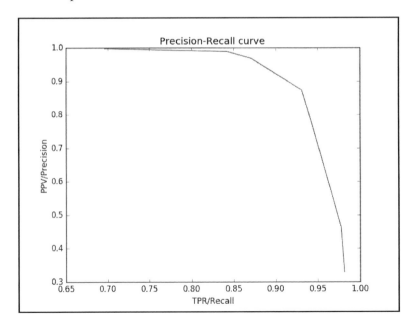

Code Structure best Practice

In previous chapters we encapsulated our tensorflow graph into a class without discussing it any further. This idea itself is already good coding practice. Having a class responsible to build your graph and exposing only things that are useful for using the model (that is, it's inputs/outputs) is a good programming practice that will save you lots of time.

Singleton Pattern

It is also common practice to use design patterns in order to solve some software design problems. One of the simplest and most useful design patterns in python is the singleton one. It is used when you want to force the instantiation of a class to only one object, so even if you instantiate this class multiple times in several different places in your project, you will be referencing the same object. In our case if we ask TensorFlow to create multiple nodes or graphs with the same name, it will throw an error. Therefore, we use the singleton pattern while creating the graph to avoid building it twice.

In the following example we summarize a simple classification model while also ensuring that the graph will not be built multiple times (aka Singleton pattern).

Pay attention to the definition of the __new__ class method. In Python, __new__ will be called when we create a new instance of a class.

```
class CAE_CNN_Encoder(object):
    __instance = None

    # Singleton pattern
    def __new__(cls):
        if CAE_CNN_Encoder.__instance is None:
            # First time new is called
            CAE_CNN_Encoder.__instance = object.__new__(cls)
            CAE_CNN_Encoder.__instance.build_graph()
        return CAE_CNN_Encoder.__instance

    def build_graph(self, img_size=28):
        self.__x = tf.placeholder(tf.float32, shape=[None, img_size *
img_size], name='IMAGE_IN')
        self.__x_image = tf.reshape(self.__x, [-1, img_size, img_size, 1])
        self.__y_ = tf.placeholder("float", shape=[None, 10], name='Y')

        with tf.name_scope('ENCODER'):
            ##### ENCODER
            # CONV1: Input 28x28x1 after CONV 5x5 P:2 S:2 H_out: 1 +
(28+4-5)/2 = 14, W_out= 1 + (28+4-5)/2 = 14
```

```python
        self.__conv1_act = tf.layers.conv2d(inputs=self.__x_image,
strides=(2, 2), name='conv1',
                                            filters=16, kernel_size=[5,
5], padding="same", activation=tf.nn.relu)

        # CONV2: Input 14x14x16 after CONV 5x5 P:0 S:2 H_out: 1 +
(14+4-5)/2 = 7, W_out= 1 + (14+4-5)/2 = 7
        self.__conv2_act = tf.layers.conv2d(inputs=self.__conv1_act,
strides=(2, 2), name='conv2',
                                            filters=32, kernel_size=[5,
5], padding="same", activation=tf.nn.relu)

    with tf.name_scope('LATENT'):
        # Reshape: Input 7x7x32 after [7x7x32]
        self.__enc_out = tf.layers.flatten(self.__conv2_act,
name='flatten_conv2')
        self.__dense = tf.layers.dense(inputs=self.__enc_out, units=200,
activation=tf.nn.relu, name='fc1')
        self.__logits = tf.layers.dense(inputs=self.__dense, units=10,
name='logits')

    def __init__(self, img_size=28):
        if CAE_CNN_Encoder.__instance is None:
            self.build_graph(img_size)

    @property
    def output(self):
        return self.__logits

    @property
    def labels(self):
        return self.__y_

    @property
    def input(self):
        return self.__x

    @property
    def image_in(self):
        return self.__x_image
```

Recipe for CNN creation

The following points are based on our experience of training neural networks and of what is considered as current best practices from researchers in this field. Hopefully, they will help you if you ever need to design your own CNN architecture from scratch. But before trying out designing your own CNN, you should check out other off-the-shelf architectures to learn from them and also check if they already do the job for you.

1. Use convolution layers with kernels of size 3x3. Larger kernels are more expensive in terms of both parameters and computation. On top of this, as we saw in the earlier chapters, you can stack conv layers to produce a bigger receptive field and with the benefit of more nonlinear activations.

2. First layer convolutions should generally have at least 32 filters. This way, deeper layers are not restricted by the number of features that the first layer extracted.

3. Try to avoid the use of pooling layers, if possible. Instead, use convolution layers with strides of 2. This will downsample our inputs like pooling but it doesn't just throw away valuable information like pooling does. Also, using strided convolutions is like combining conv and pooling together in one layer.

4. When you decrease the spatial size of your feature maps, you should increase the number of filters you use so that you don't lose too much information too quickly. In deep networks, avoid reducing the spatial size too quickly in the first layers.

5. Follow the advice in this chapter about starting your network design as small and then gradually increasing the complexity so that you avoid overfitting issues.

6. Use batchnorm. It really helps with training your networks!

7. Gradually decrease the spatial size of your feature maps as you get deeper into your network.

8. Minimize the number of FC layers (use dropout before the final layer). Use FC only if you need to concatenate some scalar features in the end. (You can even avoid that by encoding things on the input channel)

9. If you require a large receptive field (detection or classification where object size is closer to the total image size), try using dilated convolutions with exponential dilation factor for each layer. This way, you will grow your receptive field very quickly while keeping the number of parameters low.

10. If the network becomes deep and training loss does not decrease, then consider using residual connections.

11. After you have your network accuracy within expected values, and if computation cost is an issue, then you might look at techniques like depthwise convolution, bottleneck modules, or whatever is coming out on the field, depending on the use case.

 Remember that training and designing CNNs is a very empirical science so always be aware that what is considered as best practices can change quickly.

Summary

In this chapter we have learnt that following best practices will help on day to day activities as a Machine Learning engineer. We have seen how to prepare and split a dataset into subsets in order to facilitate proper training and fine tuning of a network. In addition we have looked at performing meaningful tests where the results achieved are representative of the ones that we will see when the model is deployed on the target application. Another topic that has been covered is overfitting and underfitting to data and what the best practices to follow are in order to address these issues. Furthermore, the problem of imbalanced datasets was addressed and we have seen a simple example of where this might be found (disease diagnosis). To solve this problem it was suggested to collect more data, augment the dataset and select evaluation metrics that are invariant to imbalanced datasets. Lastly, it was shown how to structure code in order to make it more readable and reusable.

In the next chapter we will see how to manage large datasets and how to scale the training process to multiple GPUs and systems.

Training at Scale 9

So far in this book, the datasets we have used or looked at have ranged in size from the tens of thousands (MNIST) of samples to just over a million (ImageNet). Although all these datasets were considered huge when they first came out, and required state-of-the-art machines to use, the great speed at which technologies such as GPUs and cloud computing have advanced has now made them both easy and quick to train by people with relatively low-power machines.

However, some of the amazing power of deep neural networks comes from their ability to scale with the amount of data fed to them. In simple terms, this means that the more good, clean data you can use to train your model, the better the result is going to be. Researchers are aware of this, and we can see that the number of training samples in new public datasets has continued to increase.

As a result of this, it is highly likely that, if you start working on problems in the industry or maybe even just the latest Kaggle competition, you are likely going to be using datasets that can be many millions of elements in size. How to handle datasets this large, and also how to train your models efficiently, then becomes a real problem. The difference can mean waiting three days instead of 1 month for your model to finish training, so it isn't something you want to get wrong.

In this chapter, you will learn about some of the ways in which we can deal with the following problems:

- Having a dataset too big to fit into memory
- How to scale your training across multiple machines
- Having data too complex to be organized in normal directory folders and subfolders

Storing data in TFRecords

Let's start by considering the example of training a network for image classification. In this case, our data will be a collection of images with an associated label. One way we might store our data is in a directory-like structure of folders. For each label, we will have a folder containing the images belonging to that label:

```
-Data
 - Person
    -im1.png
 - Cat
    -im2.png
 - Dog
    -im3.png
```

Although this might seem a simple way to store our data, it has some major drawbacks as soon as the dataset size becomes too big. One big disadvantage comes when we start loading it.

Opening a file is a time-consuming operation, and having to open many millions of files multiple times is going to add a large overhead to training time. On top of this, as we have our data all split up, it is not going to be in one nice block of memory. The hard drive is going to have to do even more work trying to locate and access them all.

What is the solution? We put them all into a single file. The advantage of doing this is that all your data will be better aligned in your computer memory for reading, which will speed things up. Having everything in one file also means that we don't have to spend time loading many millions of files, which would be extremely slow and inefficient.

There are several different formats we can use to store our data as we want, such as HDF5 or LMDB. However, as we are using TensorFlow, we will go ahead and use its own built-in format called TFRecords. TFRecords is TensorFlow's own standard file format for storing your data. It is a binary file format providing sequential access to its contents. It is flexible enough that we can store complicated datasets and labels along with any metadata we might want as well.

Making a TFRecord

Before we start, let's break down how a TFRecord works. After you open a TFRecord file for writing, you create something called an Example. This is just a protocol buffer that we will use to stuff all the data we want to save inside. Within an Example, we will store our data in Features. Features is a way to describe the data inside of our Example. A Feature can be one of three types: bytes list, float list, or int64 list. Once we have put all our data into the Features and written them into the Example buffer, we will serialize the whole protocol buffer to a string and then this is what we write to the TFRecord file.

Let's see how this can work in practice. We will keep using our previous example of image classification and create a TFRecord to store the relevant data.

First, we create our file, and this will also return to us a way to write to it:

```
writer = tf.python_io.TFRecordWriter('/data/dataset.tfrecord')
```

Next, we are going to assume that our images have been loaded and are in memory as a numpy array already; we will see later how we can store encoded images as well:

```
# labels is a list of integer labels.
# image_data is an NxHxWxC numpy array of images
for index in range(len(labels)):
    image_raw = image_data[index, ...].tobytes()
# Create our feature.
    my_features= {
                'image_raw':
tf.train.Feature(bytes_list=tf.train.BytesList(value=[image_raw])),
'label':
 tf.train.Feature(int64_list=tf.train.Int64List(value=[labels[index]]))}
    # The Example protocol buffer.
    example =
tf.train.Example(features=tf.train.Features(feature=my_features)
    writer.write(example.SerializeToString())

  writer.close()  # Close our tfrecord file after finishing writing to it.
```

We loop over the list of labels, converting each image array to raw bytes one at a time.

To store data in our example, we need to add Features to it. We store our Features in a dictionary where each key is some string name we choose, for instance, `label`, and the value is a `tf.train.Feature`, which will be our data.

The data going into the `tf.train.Feature` must be converted to the correct type that it expects using either `tf.train.BytesList, tf.train.Int64List,` or `tf.train.FloatList`.

Next, we create a `tf.train.Example` protocol buffer and pass the Features to it. Finally, we serialize our Example to string and write it to our TFRecord file. Once we have looped through the whole array of images, we must remember to close our file for writing.

Storing encoded images

One option to optimize memory usage is to encode the images using some sort of compression (that is, PNG) on this case the TFRecord will be smaller, but you still need to uncompress the data before use, which may take some time. What is done in practice is to use another CPU core to alleviate computing.

Sharding

Although we said that it is best if we have all our data in one file, this is not actually 100% true. As TFRecords are read sequentially, we are unable to shuffle our dataset if we use just one file. Every time you reach the end of the TFRecord after an epoch of training, you will go back to the start of the dataset but, unfortunately, the data will be in the same order every time you go through the file.

In order to allow us to shuffle data, one thing we can do is *shard* our data by creating multiple TFRecord files and spreading out data across these multiple files. This way, we can just shuffle the order that we load the TFRecord files each epoch and thus our data will be effectively shuffled for us while we train. Something like 1,000 shards for every million images is a good baseline to follow.

In the next section, we will see how to use our TFRecords to make efficient data feeding pipelines.

Making efficient pipelines

When we dealt with smaller datasets, it was enough for us to just load the entire dataset into computer memory. This is simple and works fine if your dataset is small enough; however, a lot of the time, this won't be the case. We will now look at how to overcome this issue.

In order to avoid loading all our data at once, we will need to create a data pipeline that can feed our training data to the model. This pipeline will be responsible for, among other things, loading a batch of elements from storage, preprocessing the data, and finally, feeding the data to our model. Luckily for us, this can all be easily accomplished using the TensorFlow data API.

For these examples, we are going to assume that we have saved our data into multiple (two in this case) TFRecord files like those described previously. There is no difference if you have more than two; you just have to include all their names when setting things up.

We start by creating a TFRecord dataset from a list of all the TFRecord file names:

```
# Create a TFRecord dataset that reads all of the Examples from
  two files.
train_filenames= ["/data/train1.tfrecord", "/data/train2.tfrecord"]
train_dataset = tf.data.TFRecordDataset(filenames)
```

Next, we have to decode our TFRecords. To do this, we write a function that will take in a TFRecord, decode it and then return an input image and its corresponding label:

```
# Function for decoding our TFRecord. We assume our images are fixed size
224x224x3
 def decode_tfrec(proto_in):

    my_features = {'image_raw': tf.FixedLenFeature([], tf.string),
               'Label': tf.FixedLenFeature([], tf.int64)}
    parsed_features = tf.parse_single_example(proto_in,
features=my_features)image = tf.decode_raw(parsed_features['image_raw'],
tf.uint8)
    image = tf.cast(image, tf.float32)  # Tensorflow data needs to be
float32.
    image = tf.reshape(image, [224,224,3])  # Need to reshape your images.

    label = tf.cast(parsed_features['label'], tf.int32)  # Labels need to
be int32

    label = tf.one_hot(label, depth=...)  # Convert our labels to one hot.
 return image, label
```

We then pass this function to the `dataset.map()` method, which will execute it for us:

```
train_dataset = train_dataset.map(decode_tfrec, num_parallel_calls=4)
```

Parallel calls for map transformations

Any map transformation you call on your dataset by default acts only on a single element of your dataset, and it will process elements sequentially. The easiest thing you can do to speed things up and use all your CPU power is to set the `num_parallel_calls` argument to the number of CPU cores you have available to you. This way, we don't waste any CPU power available to us. You are warned, however, not to set this higher than the number of cores available to you, as this may actually reduce performance because of inefficient scheduling.

Any transformations you want to do to your data, such as data augmentations, can also be written as functions and then passed to the map method as before, to apply them to the dataset. For example, note the following code:

```
train_dataset = train_dataset.map(decode_tfrec, num_parallel_calls=4)  #
Decode tfrecord.
 train_dataset = train_dataset.map(data_augmentation,
 num_parallel_calls=4)  # Augment data.
```

Getting a batch

The final thing you want to do at the end of your pipeline is to produce a batch of data ready to send to your GPU for training. This is done simply with the batch method and passing in the size of batch you want:

```
train_dataset = train_dataset.batch(128)  # Take a batch of 128 from the
dataset.
```

The size of the batch is an important parameter when trying to make our pipeline as efficient as possible; having it as large as possible may not always be best. For example, if you have lots of preprocessing steps on your images, then your GPU may be standing idle while your CPU does preprocessing for a large batch of images, getting them ready.

Prefetching

Another way we can make an efficient data pipeline is by always having a batch of data ready to send to the GPU. Ideally, when training our model, we would like our GPU usage to be at 100% all the time. This way, we are making the maximum usage of our expensive piece of hardware that is efficiently computing forward and backward passes while training.

For this to happen though, we need our CPUs to load and prepare a batch of images, ready to pass to the GPU, during the time it takes to do a forward and backward pass of the model. Luckily, we can do this easily using a simple prefetch transformation after we collect our batch, as follows:

```
train_dataset= train_dataset.batch(128).prefetch(1)
```

Using prefetch will make sure our data pipeline prepares a whole batch of data for us, while training is happening, ready to be loaded into the GPU for the next iteration. Doing this ensures that our pipeline is not slowed waiting for a batch to be collected, and if fetching a batch takes less time than a forward and backward pass of the model, then our pipeline will be as efficient as it can be.

To be clear, using `prefetch(1)` here means that we `prefetch` the whole batch of data. This is why, we have batching as the last step in the pipeline and use the prefetch here as doing so is most effective.

Tracing your graph

TensorFlow provides a nice way to profile and see how long your whole graph takes to execute through its timeline tracing tool. This is a great tool to see what parts of your graph are slowing down your training and to spot any inefficiencies in your data pipeline.

We will start by giving you an example of how to trace your graph. It is quite simple: you just add a couple of extra lines to your normal code and a JSON file will be produced that we can load in the Google Chrome browser to see all the timings of the graph execution:

```
from tensorflow.python.client import timeline
.... # Your model and training code here
with tf.Session() as sess:

    # We set some options to give to the session so graph execution is
profiled.
    options = tf.RunOptions(trace_level=tf.RunOptions.FULL_TRACE)
    run_metadata = tf.RunMetadata()
    # Run your graph and supply the options we set.
    sess.run(model_output, options=options, run_metadata=run_metadata)
   # We create the Timeline object here then write it to json file.
    created_timeline = timeline.Timeline(run_metadata.step_stats)
    chome_readable_trace = created_timeline.generate_chrome_trace_format()

    with open('my_timeline.json', 'w') as file:
        file.write(chome_readable_trace)
```

In this code, we import the TensorFlow timeline module, then we set two options to enable tracing of the graph and supply them to `Session.run()`. After running the graph, we create the `Timeline` object that will contain the results of profiling the graph execution. We then convert this to Chrome trace format and finally write it to a JSON file.

To see the results, you need to open up a new Chrome window. Then, type in `chrome://tracing` in the address bar and press *Enter*. There will be a load button in the top-left corner. Use this to load the JSON file you just saved.

The results of tracing your graph will now be displayed. Looking at this will tell you how long each part of your graph took to execute. You should pay particular attention to where there are large blocks of white space. These white spaces indicate where devices, such as your GPU, are sitting waiting for data so that they can perform calculations. You should try and eliminate these by optimizing the way you feed data.

Note, however, that your pipeline may be completely optimized, but you don't have CPU cycles to process the pipeline fast enough. Check your CPU usage to see if this is the case.

Distributed computing in TensorFlow

In this section, you will learn how to distribute computation in TensorFlow; the importance of knowing how to do this is highlighted as follows:

- Run more experiments in parallel (namely, finding hyperparameters, for example, gridsearch)
- Distribute model training over multiple GPUs (on multiple servers) to reduce training time

One famous use case was when Facebook published a paper that was able to train ImageNet in 1 hour (instead of weeks). Basically, it trained a ResNet-50 on ImageNet on 256 GPUs, distributed on 32 servers, with a batch size of 8,192 images.

Model/data parallelism

There are mainly two ways to achieve parallelism and scale your task in multiple servers:

- **Model Parallelism**: When your model does not fit on the GPU, you need to compute layers on different servers.

- **Data Parallelism**: When we have the same model distributed on different servers but handling different batches, so each server will have a different gradient and we need some sort of synchronization between the servers.

In this section, we will focus on data parallelism, which is simple for implementation:

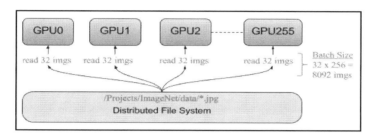

Synchronous/asynchronous SGD

As mentioned before, in data parallelism, each model will grab some data from the training set and calculate their own gradient, but somehow we need to synchronize a way before updating the model, given that each worker will have the same model.

In synchronous SGD, all workers calculate a gradient and wait to have all gradients calculated, then the model is updated and distributed to all the workers again:

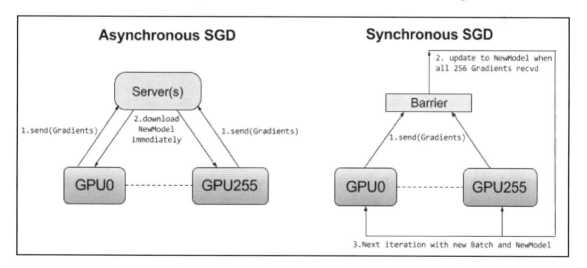

When data does not fit on one computer

One problem that may occur is that we simply can't store the data on one computer and/or we still need to search for things on this dataset. To solve this kind of problem, we may need distributed **Not only SQL (NoSQL)** databases, such as Cassandra. Cassandra supports data distribution on multiple systems where availability and performance are critical:

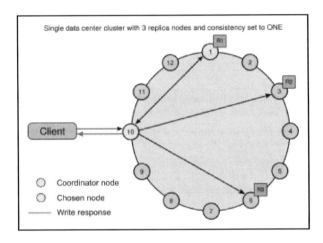

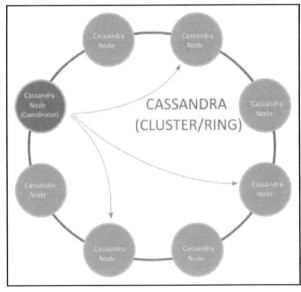

Cassandra tries its best to not have a single point of failure. For example, all nodes will act like a sort of master (there is no actual master) so that all nodes have the responsibility to handle requests and automatically distribute data between nodes, in some sort of high-availability backup.

The advantages of NoSQL systems

NoSQL databases, in contrast with relational databases (such as older versions of MySQL and PostgreSQL), shine when the amount of data becomes too big, and also when we don't need the Features of relational databases (such as triggers or stored procedures).

Before we continue, let's list out the advantages of NoSQL systems:

- Scale horizontally; to get more performance, just add more machines
- We don't need to know in advance the relations between tables
- Allow changing tables structure while the whole thing is working
- Faster (no complex relational database mechanism)
- Data is normally saved on distributed filesystems, so, for example, storing images in NoSQL databases is fine

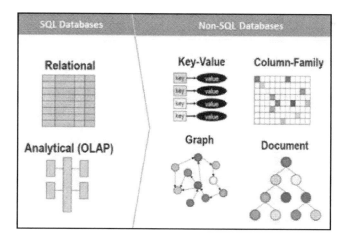

Installing Cassandra (Ubuntu 16.04)

Install Oracle Java 1.8:

- `sudo apt-get update`

- sudo add-apt-repository ppa:webupd8team/java
- sudo apt-get update
- sudo apt-get -y install oracle-java8-installer

Install Cassandra:

- echo "deb http://www.apache.org/dist/Cassandra/debian 310x main" | sudo tee -a /etc/apt/sources.list.d/cassandra.sources.list
- curl https://www.apache.org/dist/Cassandra/KEYS | sudo apt-key add -
- sudo apt-get update
- sudo apt-get install cassandra
- sudo service cassandra status
- sudo nodetool status

The CQLSH tool

CQLSH is a tool that allows you to issue SQL commands to Cassandra nodes:

For Graphical User Interface, there is a nice tool called DBWeaver that also does the job:

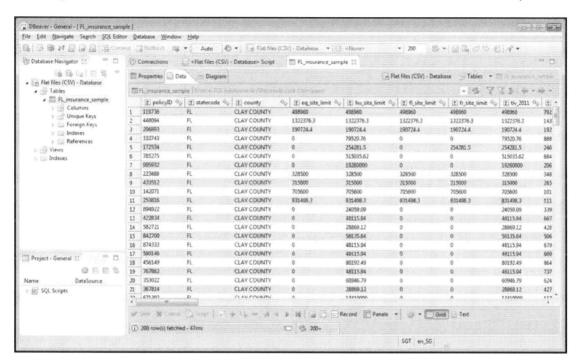

DBWeaver Sample

Creating databases, tables, and indexes

1. First, we need to create the database (keyspace) and choose how our nodes will replicate the data:

```
CREATE KEYSPACE mydb WITH REPLICATION = { 'class' :
'SimpleStrategy', 'replication_factor' : 1 };
```

2. Now, we create a table:

```
CREATE TABLE tb_drive ( id uuid PRIMARY KEY, wheel_angle float, acc
float, image blob );
```

3. Add some data as follows:

```
INSERT INTO tb_drive (id,wheel_angle,acc) VALUES (now(),0.2,0.5);
INSERT INTO tb_drive (id,wheel_angle,acc) VALUES (now(),0.1,0.5);
INSERT INTO tb_drive (id,wheel_angle,acc) VALUES (now(),0.0,0.5);
```

4. Create indexes (at any point in time) to all the columns that you want to query (that's why is fast):

```
CREATE INDEX idxAngle ON tb_drive (wheel_angle);
CREATE INDEX idxAcc ON tb_drive (acc);
```

Doing queries in Python

First, before we start playing around, we need to install the Python driver `pip install cassandra-driver`; the following snippet of code just lists the content of a table in the Cassandra cluster:

```python
from cassandra.cluster import Cluster
import cassandra.util
import uuid
import numpy as np

# Considering that the cluster is on localhost
cluster = Cluster()
# Other option if you know the IPs
# cluster = Cluster(['192.168.0.1', '192.168.0.2'])
# Get a session to the database
session = cluster.connect('mydb')

# Doing a query
rows = session.execute('SELECT * FROM tb_drive limit 5')
print('Columns:',rows.column_names)
for row in rows:
    print(row.id, row.acc, row.wheel_angle)
```

Populating tables in Python

In the following example, we will populate our table, including a field that stores images:

```python
insert_string = """INSERT INTO tb_drive (id, wheel_angle, acc, image)
VALUES (%s, %s, %s, %s)"""
for data in dataset:
    # Split from dataset the image path, steering angle, and acceleration
```

```
    img_path, steering_angle, acc = data
    # Load image (png compressed)
    with open(img_path, 'rb') as f:
        content_file = f.read()

    # Insert into database
    session.execute(insert_string,(uuid.uuid1(), steering_angle, acc,
content_file))
```

Doing backups

For backups (snapshots): Results stored in `var/lib/cassandra/data/`):

```
nodetool -h localhost snapshot mydb
```

For restoring the data (where you may need to truncate/delete the table), perform the following:

We then copy the snapshot (database backup file) created before the directory: `/var/lib/Cassandra/data/keyspace/table_name-UUID` and then:

```
nodetool refresh
```

Scaling computation in the cloud

During your design cycle and life as a machine learning engineer, you may face occasions where the amount of computation power available at your office is simply not enough, and you can't wait for your IT team to buy you a new server. So, for example, if you can afford 24.48 dollars/hour, you may have a p3.16xlarge with 8 GPUs Nvidia V100, 64 cores, and 488 GB of RAM.

In this section, you will learn about Amazon AWS services that might help you deal with a lack of computing power issues.

You will learn about the following Amazon Cloud Services:

- **Elastic Compute Cloud (EC2)**
- S3
- SageMaker

EC2

This is the service where we create our servers, where you basically create any server to do your work:

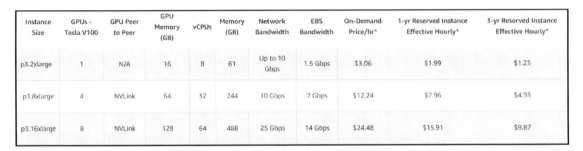

Instance Size	GPUs - Tesla V100	GPU Peer to Peer	GPU Memory (GB)	vCPUs	Memory (GB)	Network Bandwidth	EBS Bandwidth	On-Demand Price/hr*	1-yr Reserved Instance Effective Hourly*	3-yr Reserved Instance Effective Hourly*
p3.2xlarge	1	N/A	16	8	61	Up to 10 Gbps	1.5 Gbps	$3.06	$1.99	$1.23
p3.8xlarge	4	NVLink	64	32	244	10 Gbps	7 Gbps	$12.24	$7.96	$4.93
p3.16xlarge	8	NVLink	128	64	488	25 Gbps	14 Gbps	$24.48	$15.91	$9.87

Here, you configure stuff like how you want to access your server (normally with a private key):

Here, we configure how much disk space we want:

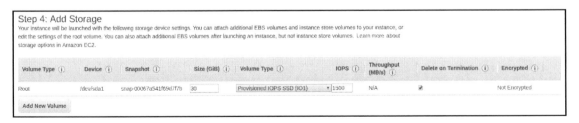

And here, we configure the ports that are going to be available:

Available ports

AMI

This is one of the coolest Features in AWS, and it allows you to create images from all data and installed tools from one server instance into another. So, you can just configure one server with all tools, drivers, and so on, and in the future, use a different server with the same image:

Storage (S3)

Amazon S3 is the storage system from where you can upload/download files (from normal HTTP requests). S3 is organized with the idea of *buckets* from which you may store/download files. Also, there are plugins that allow you to map S3 directly to your EC2 instance like some remote folder (which is not recommended):

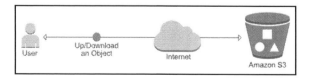

The following screenshot shows how to create a bucket:

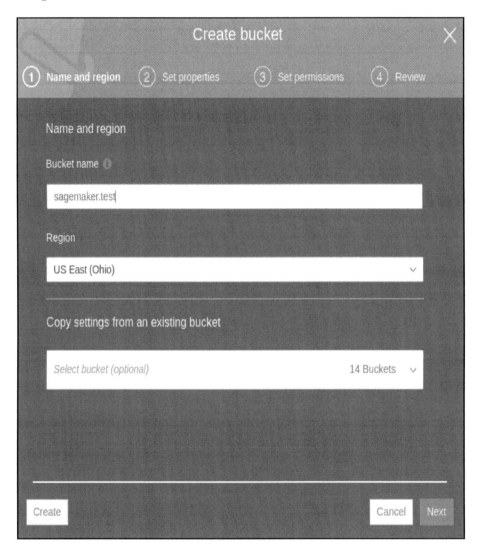

The S3 system can be configured publicly, so people can download/upload stuff from anywhere.

SageMaker

SageMaker provides an easy way to train/deploy machine learning models in the cloud. SageMaker will provide a Jupyter notebook, where you can visualize/train your models and connect directly to data from S3 (API to access S3 is provided):

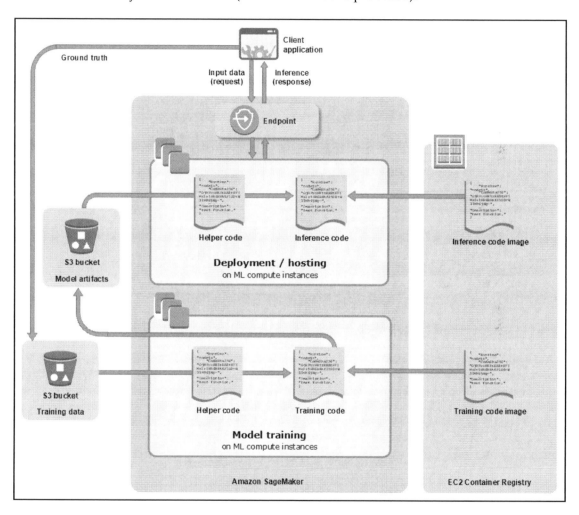

Here, we show the default options to create a notebook instance:

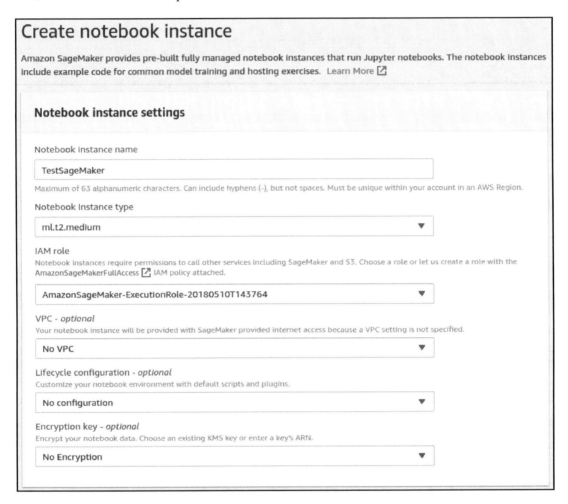

Here is the notebook panel:

And, here is the notebook (you can see examples of training models to check how the API works):

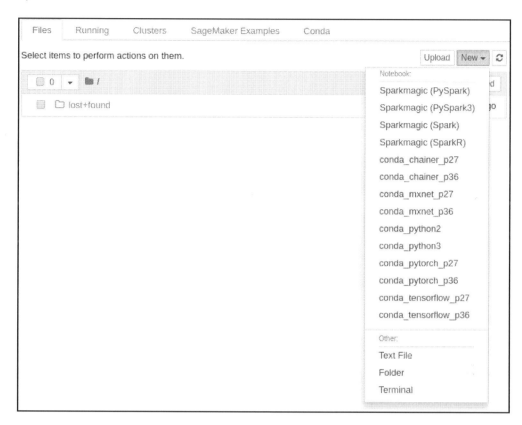

Summary

In this chapter, you learned how to deal with having datasets that are too big to be handled by your normal desktop computer. We saw how to train TensorFlow models across multiple GPUs and machines, and finally, we looked at best practices for storing your data and feeding it to your model efficiently.

Over the course of this book, we have looked at many of the current popular problems in computer vision and how deep learning can be used to tackle all of them. We have also provided insight into how these might be implemented in TensorFlow. Along the way, we gave an introduction to how to use TensorFlow.

References

Chapter 1

Here we're going to learn how to install and the basics of Tensorflow, as references we have:

- https://www.tensorflow.org/tutorials/
- https://www.tensorflow.org/install/

Chapter 2

This chapter will tackle the principals of Machine Learning and Neural Networks with emphasis on Computer Vision with Convolutional Neural Networks. The references for the chapter are:

- https://en.wikipedia.org/wiki/Artificial_neural_network
- https://en.wikipedia.org/wiki/Timeline_of_machine_learning
- http://ais.informatik.uni-freiburg.de/teaching/ss11/ki/slides/ai12_acting_under_uncertainty_handout_4up.pdf
- http://yann.lecun.com/exdb/publis/pdf/lecun-98.pdf
- https://www.facebook.com/yann.lecun/posts/10152820758292143
- https://towardsdatascience.com/types-of-convolutions-in-deep-learning-717013397f4d
- http://cs231n.stanford.edu/
- http://cs224d.stanford.edu/

Chapter 3

This chapter will be cover image classification using Deep learning, and why CNNs disrupted the way we do computer vision now. The references for this chapter are:

- `Learning Multiple Layers of Features from Tiny Images`, Alex Krizhevsky, 2009

- An excellent flashback on image representation techniques can be found in the *Computer Vision: Algorithms and Applications*, Richard Szeliski, 2010

- `http://www.vision.caltech.edu/Image_Datasets/Caltech101/`

- Griffin, Gregory and Holub, Alex and Perona, Pietro (2007) Caltech–256 *Object Category Dataset*

- Everingham, M., Van Gool, L., Williams, C. K. I., Winn, J. and Zisserman, *A International Journal of Computer Vision*, 88(2), 303-338, 2010

- *ImageNet Large Scale Visual Recognition Challenge*, IJCV, 2015

- `https://wordnet.princeton.edu/`

- *What Does Classifying More Than 10,000 Image Categories Tell Us?* Jia Deng, Alexander C. Berg, Kai Li, and Li Fei-Fei

- Olga Russakovsky, Jia Deng et al. (2015) *ImageNet Large Scale Visual Recognition Challenge*, `https://arxiv.org/pdf/1409.0575.pdf`

- Alex Krizhevsky, Ilya Sutskever and Geoffrey Hinton, *ImageNet Classification with Deep Convolutional Neural Networks*, 2012

- `https://arxiv.org/pdf/1311.2901.pdf`

- *Going deeper with convolutions* by Christian Szegedy Google Inc. et al

- *Deep Residual Learning for Image Recognition*, Kaiming He et al.

- `https://arxiv.org/pdf/1709.01507.pdf`

- The batch norm paper is a really well written paper that is easy to understand and explains the concept in much more detail, `https://arxiv.org/pdf/1502.03167.pdf`

Chapter 4

In this chapter we will learn about object detection and segmentation. The references for this chapter are:

- `https://arxiv.org/pdf/1311.2524.pdf` (*Rich feature hierarchies for accurate object detection and semantic segmentation*)
- `https://arxiv.org/pdf/1504.08083.pdf` (*Fast RCNN*)
- `https://arxiv.org/pdf/1506.01497.pdf` (*Faster RCNN Towards Real-Time Object Detection with Region Proposals*)
- `https://www.youtube.com/watch?v=v5bFVbQvFRk`
- `https://arxiv.org/pdf/1506.02640.pdf` (*You Only Look Once: Unified, Real-Time Object Detection*)
- `https://coursera.org/specializations/deep-learning` (*Deep Learning* course by Andrew Ng)
- `https://people.eecs.berkeley.edu/~jonlong/long_shelhamer_fcn.pdf` (*Fully Convolutional Neural Network for Semantic Segmentation*)
- `https://arxiv.org/pdf/1606.00915.pdf` (Semantic Image Segmentation with Deep Convolutional Nets, Atrous Convolution, and Fully Connected CRFs)

Chapter 5

In this chapter we will learn about some common CNN architectures (that is, VGG, ResNet, GoogleNet). The references for this chapter are:

- Simonyan, K. and Zisserman, A., 2014, *Very Deep Convolutional Networks for Large-Scale Image Recognition,* `arXiv preprint arXiv:1409.1556`
- *Going Deeper With Convolutions,* `https://arxiv.org/abs/1409.4842`
- *Deep Residual Learning for Image Recognition,* Kaiming He, Xiangyu Zhang, Shaoqing Ren, Jian Sun, Microsoft Research
- *Mobilenets: Efficient Convolutional Neural Networks for Mobile Vision Applications,* `https://arxiv.org/abs/1704.04861`
- `https://arxiv.org/pdf/1801.04381.pdf,` MobileNets V2

Chapter 7

This chapter will discuss transfer learning and how we can take advantage of other people's model training to help us train our own networks. The references for this chapter are:

- `https://www.cse.ust.hk/~qyang/Docs/2009/tkde_transfer_learning.pdf`
- `ftp://ftp.cs.wisc.edu/machine-learning/shavlik-group/torrey.handbook09.pdf`
- `https://arxiv.org/pdf/1403.6382.pdf` (*CNN Features off-the-shelf: an Astounding Baseline for Recognition*)
- `https://arxiv.org/pdf/1310.1531.pdf` (*DeCAF: A Deep Convolutional Activation Feature for Generic Visual Recognition*)

Chapter 9

In the last chapter of this book we will learn how to take advantage of parallel cluster of computers in the cloud to accelerate model training. The references for this chapter are:

- `https://www.oreilly.com/ideas/distributed-tensorflow`
- `https://research.fb.com/wp-content/uploads/2017/06/imagenet1kin1h5.pdf`
- `https://learningtensorflow.com/lesson11/`
- `https://www.tensorflow.org/deploy/distributed`
- `https://www.tensorflow.org/programmers_guide/low_level_intro`
- `https://github.com/tmulc18/Distributed-TensorFlow-Guide`
- `https://clusterone.com/blog/2017/09/13/distributed-tensorflow-clusterone/`
- `https://www.youtube.com/watch?v=-h0cWBiQ8s8`
- `https://www.youtube.com/watch?v=uIcqeP7MFH0`
- `https://www.youtube.com/watch?v=bRMGoPqsn20`
- `https://www.youtube.com/watch?v=1cHx1baKqq0`

Other Books You May Enjoy

If you enjoyed this book, you may be interested in these other books by Packt:

Deep Learning with TensorFlow - Second Edition
Giancarlo Zaccone, Md. Rezaul Karim

ISBN: 9781788831109

- Apply deep machine intelligence and GPU computing with TensorFlow
- Access public datasets and use TensorFlow to load, process, and transform the data
- Discover how to use the high-level TensorFlow API to build more powerful applications
- Use deep learning for scalable object detection and mobile computing
- Train machines quickly to learn from data by exploring reinforcement learning techniques
- Explore active areas of deep learning research and applications

Natural Language Processing with TensorFlow
Thushan Ganegedara

ISBN: 9781788478311

- Core concepts of NLP and various approaches to natural language processing
- How to solve NLP tasks by applying TensorFlow functions to create neural networks
- Strategies to process large amounts of data into word representations that can be used by deep learning applications
- Techniques for performing sentence classification and language generation using CNNs and RNNs
- About employing state-of-the art advanced RNNs, like long short-term memory, to solve complex text generation tasks
- How to write automatic translation programs and implement an actual neural machine translator from scratch
- The trends and innovations that are paving the future in NLP

Leave a review - let other readers know what you think

Please share your thoughts on this book with others by leaving a review on the site that you bought it from. If you purchased the book from Amazon, please leave us an honest review on this book's Amazon page. This is vital so that other potential readers can see and use your unbiased opinion to make purchasing decisions, we can understand what our customers think about our products, and our authors can see your feedback on the title that they have worked with Packt to create. It will only take a few minutes of your time, but is valuable to other potential customers, our authors, and Packt. Thank you!

Index

Made in the USA
San Bernardino, CA
07 February 2019